MW01602356

From Zero to Meme Coin Hero

A Step-by-Step Playbook for Spotting and Flipping Early-Stage Tokens

Gerry Marrs Publications

Gerry Marrs Publications

Published by Gerry Marrs Publications

www.gerrymarrspublications.com

Disclaimer:

The information provided in this book, "From Zero to Meme Coin Hero: A Step-by-Step Playbook for Spotting and Flipping Early-Stage Tokens," is for educational and informational purposes only. It is not intended as, and should not be construed as, financial advice. Always conduct your own research and consult with a qualified financial advisor before making any investment decisions. The author and publisher are not responsible for any financial losses or other consequences resulting from the use of the information provided in this book.

Trademarks:

All product names, logos, and brands mentioned in this book are the property of their respective owners. Use of these names, logos, and brands does not imply endorsement.

First Edition

Printed in the United States of America

Contents

Introduction

Welcome to the fascinating world of meme coins and cryptocurrencies! In this book, we embark on a journey to explore the intriguing landscape of digital currencies, focusing specifically on the rise of meme coins and their unique place within the cryptocurrency realm.

Chapter 1 sets the stage by providing a comprehensive understanding of meme coins and their significance in the ever-evolving cryptocurrency market. We delve into the definition of meme coins, showcasing notable examples like Dogecoin and Shiba Inu, and examine how community-driven narratives and social media memes have shaped their popularity.

Furthermore, we trace the history of meme coins, uncovering their evolution and key milestones. We investigate how these coins gained traction through online humor and influencer mentions, ultimately propelling them into the spotlight.

Throughout this exploration, we draw comparisons between meme coins and traditional cryptocurrencies, highlighting the differences in purpose, technology, and community involvement. We uncover how sentiment and hype often take precedence over traditional fundamentals in the meme coin space.

The role of community in meme coins cannot be overlooked. We analyze the significance of social engagement and fan-based communities, emphasizing the importance of trust, transparency, and communication as key success factors.

Additionally, we dive into the market dynamics of meme coins, examining their volatility, liquidity, and trading patterns. We explore how narrative shifts and "meta" trends can greatly influence short-term market behavior.

Lastly, we address the legal and regulatory considerations surrounding meme coins, providing insights into the global regulatory landscape.

Join us on this captivating journey as we unravel the captivating world of meme coins and cryptocurrencies, providing you with valuable insights and perspectives along the way. Get ready to expand your knowledge and uncover the intricacies of this exciting and ever-changing digital frontier.

Why I Decided to Write This Book

As I delved into the captivating world of meme coins and cryptocurrencies, I witnessed a phenomenon that piqued my curiosity and urged me to share my insights with you. People were making serious money by participating in this dynamic digital frontier. I saw the potential for massive gains, but I also recognized the need for a comprehensive guide that provides not only an understanding of meme coins but also the broader cryptocurrency landscape. This book aims to bridge the knowledge gap and equip you with the necessary tools and insights to navigate this exciting and ever-changing market. Whether you're a seasoned investor or new to the world of cryptocurrencies, join me on this journey to uncover the intricacies of meme coins and gain a deeper understanding of the cryptocurrency landscape.

This book empowers you to take action and make informed decisions in the world of meme coins and cryptocurrencies. As you delve into the chapters, you'll gain valuable knowledge about meme coins, their history, and their differences from traditional cryptocurrencies. But it doesn't stop there. The insights and tools provided in this book will equip you to navigate the ever-changing cryptocurrency landscape with confidence.

What Can You Do With This Book

Here's what you can do with this book:

1. **Educate Yourself**: Expand your understanding of meme coins and the broader cryptocurrency landscape. Gain insights into their characteristics, trends, and the factors that influence their value.

2. **Make Informed Investment Decisions**: Armed with knowledge, you'll be better equipped to make sensible investment decisions when it comes to meme coins and other cryptocurrencies. Understand the risks involved, evaluate market conditions, and identify potential opportunities.

3. **Manage Risks**: Learn about risk management strategies specific to meme coins and cryptocurrencies. Discover how to set realistic expectations, diversify your portfolio, and navigate the volatile nature of this market.

4. **Stay Updated**: Cryptocurrency markets evolve rapidly, and new meme coins emerge frequently. Use this book as a foundation to continue your learning journey and stay informed about the latest trends, developments, and regulations in the cryptocurrency space.

By exploring the content of this book and applying the knowledge gained, you'll be better prepared to navigate the exciting and dynamic world of meme coins and cryptocurrencies, making informed decisions that align with your financial goals.

Trading in meme coins can be an incredibly lucrative endeavor for those who navigate the volatility of the market with knowledge and strategy. With the potential for exponential gains in a short period, meme coins have garnered attention as a high-risk, high-reward investment opportunity. However, it's important to approach trading in meme coins with caution and a thorough understanding of the risks involved. The rapid rise and fall of meme coins can lead to substantial profits, but they can also result in significant losses if not approached with careful consideration and risk management. It is crucial to conduct thorough research, stay updated on market trends, and set clear investment goals when venturing into meme coin trading. As with any investment, diversification and a long-term perspective are key to mitigating risks and maximizing potential returns.

Share Your Knowledge With Others

Spreading the word about meme coins and the cryptocurrency landscape is integral to building a community and fostering success in this endeavor. Social media platforms play a pivotal role in connecting individuals and amplifying trends, making them an invaluable tool for sharing knowledge and insights. By leveraging the power of social media, you can contribute to the broader conversation around meme coins and educate others about the opportunities and risks involved. Engaging with like-minded individuals, participating in relevant communities, and sharing informative content can help establish your presence and credibility in the meme coin trading sphere. Additionally, by staying active on social media, you can stay abreast of the latest trends, news, and discussions, enabling you to make more informed decisions and adapt to the ever-evolving meme coin landscape. Together, let's cultivate a knowledgeable and informed community that embraces responsible meme coin trading practices.

How Much Money Can You Make?

Meme coins have gained significant attention for their potential to generate substantial returns on investment. While it is true that some investors have seen remarkable profits, it is crucial to approach meme coin trading with caution and realistic expectations. The meme coin market is highly volatile, and prices can fluctuate dramatically in short periods. It is essential to conduct thorough research, understand the risks involved, and only invest what you can afford to lose. While it is possible to make money with meme coins, it is equally important to be prepared for potential losses. Remember, responsible trading practices and informed decision-making are key to navigating the meme coin landscape and ensuring a sustainable and successful investment journey.

Case Examples of Teens Making Profits with Meme Coins

While it is important to approach investing in meme coins with caution, there have been instances where young investors have seen significant returns. These cases serve as examples of the potential opportunities within the meme coin market. It's important to note that these examples are publicly known cases, and I do not personally know these individuals:

- **Teen Investor A:** A 17-year-old investor from the United States reportedly invested a small amount in a meme coin and saw their investment grow significantly over time. Their initial investment of a few hundred dollars turned into thousands within a few months, highlighting the potential for substantial returns.

- **Teen Investor B:** A 16-year-old investor from Canada shared their success story of making a substantial profit with a meme coin. Starting with an initial investment of a few thousand dollars, their investment grew exponentially, reaching a value of over a million dollars in just a year.

These cases demonstrate that there have been instances where young investors have made substantial profits by investing in meme coins. However, it is crucial to remember that these examples are not representative of every investor's experience, and investing in meme coins still carries significant risks. Responsible investing practices, thorough research, and understanding the volatile nature of the market are essential for anyone considering investing in meme coins.

Now, let's dive deep into the world of meme-coin trading!

Chapter 1

Understanding Meme Coins and the Cryptocurrency Landscape

Welcome to Chapter 1 of our guide on meme coins and the fascinating world of cryptocurrency. In this chapter, we will dive into the world of meme coins, exploring their definition, history, and how they differ from traditional cryptocurrencies. We will also examine the influential role of community-driven narratives and social media memes in the rise of meme coins. By the end of this chapter, you will have a better understanding of the unique characteristics and dynamics that make meme coins such an intriguing phenomenon in the cryptocurrency landscape. So, let's explore the captivating world of meme coins and uncover the factors that contribute to their popularity and volatility.

What Are Meme Coins?

Meme coins have emerged as a captivating and unique phenomenon within the world of cryptocurrencies. These digital assets, inspired by internet memes and cultural references, have gained substantial popularity and attention in recent years. At their core, meme coins are characterized by their community-driven nature, often fueled by social media platforms and online communities. Notable examples of meme coins include Dogecoin and Shiba Inu, which have garnered significant attention and market value.

The rise of meme coins can be attributed to the power of community-driven narratives and social media memes. Unlike traditional cryptocurrencies that often rely on technical advancements or real-world use cases, meme coins thrive on the collective enthusiasm and engagement of their communities. The viral nature of memes and the ability of social media platforms to quickly spread information have played a crucial role in amplifying the popularity and visibility of meme coins. As these coins become the subject of online humor and influencer mentions, their value and market dynamics can experience significant fluctuations.

When comparing meme coins to traditional cryptocurrencies, notable differences emerge. While traditional cryptocurrencies often prioritize technological advancements and real-world applications, meme coins tend to focus more on sentiment and hype. The value and success of meme coins are heavily influenced by the emotions and enthusiasm of their communities, rather than traditional financial or technological fundamentals. This unique characteristic of meme coins has led to a distinct investment landscape with greater volatility and unpredictability.

Community involvement is a vital component of meme coins. The engagement and participation of the community shape the narrative and trajectory of these coins. Social media platforms and online communities provide spaces for meme coin enthusiasts to connect, exchange ideas, and drive the direction of their chosen coin. In turn, this active community participation contributes to the hype and volatility associated with meme coins. The sense of belonging and collective identity surrounding meme coins often creates passionate and dedicated communities, further driving the popularity and success of these digital assets.

Definition and examples (e.g., Dogecoin, Shiba Inu)

The influence of community-driven narratives and social media memes has played a significant role in the rise of meme coins. Memes, with their viral nature and ability to capture collective interest and humor, have become a powerful force in shaping the trajectory of these digital assets. The communities surrounding meme coins actively engage in online platforms, such as Reddit or Discord, creating spaces for enthusiasts to connect, share ideas, and collectively drive the direction of their chosen coin. This participation and sense of belonging contribute to the hype and volatility associated with meme coins. Moreover, the passionate and dedicated communities formed around these coins further amplify their popularity, creating a fervor that propels the success of meme coins like Dogecoin and Shiba Inu.

10 Examples of Meme Coins and Their Impact

Here are 10 influential meme coins that have made their mark in the cryptocurrency space:

1. **Dogecoin (DOGE):** Originally created as a joke in 2013, Dogecoin gained a massive following due to its iconic Shiba Inu dog logo. It has since become one of the most well-known meme coins and has experienced significant price surges driven by online communities.

2. **Shiba Inu (SHIB):** Inspired by Dogecoin, Shiba Inu gained popularity as an experimental project aiming to create a decentralized ecosystem. Its online community, known as the "ShibArmy," has played a crucial role in driving its adoption and price fluctuations.

3. **SafeMoon (SAFEMOON):** SafeMoon gained attention for its unique tokenomics, including a deflationary mechanism. Its dedicated community actively promotes and trades the coin, contributing to its market volatility.

4. **Elon Musk (EMC2):** Named after the Tesla CEO himself, Elon Musk coin gained popularity due to its association with the influential entrepreneur. The community behind this meme coin often engages in discussions related to Musk's tweets and actions.

5. **Baby Doge Coin (BABYDOGE):** Baby Doge Coin gained traction as a spin-off of Dogecoin, capitalizing on the popularity of the Doge meme. Its community embraces the "Hodl" mentality and actively supports charitable causes.

6. **Safemoon Cash (SAFEMOONCASH):** Safemoon Cash emerged as a fork of SafeMoon, aiming to offer a similar tokenomics structure. Its community actively discusses and promotes the coin on various social media platforms.

7. **Hoge Finance (HOGE):** Hoge Finance gained attention for its decentralized finance (DeFi) ecosystem and unique features such as auto-staking. Its community actively champions the coin's growth and development.

8. **Floki Inu (FLOKI):** Inspired by Elon Musk's pet dog, Floki Inu garnered attention for its association with the Tesla CEO. The community behind Floki Inu actively engages in online discussions, driving interest and awareness.

9. **Kishu Inu (KISHU):** Kishu Inu gained popularity as a meme coin with a charitable focus. Its community, known as "Kishu Army," actively supports animal welfare organizations and promotes the coin's adoption.

10. **Ass Coin (ASS):** Ass Coin gained attention for its unique and catchy name, which resonated with the online meme culture. Its community actively engages in online discussions and promotions, contributing to its visibility and popularity.

These meme coins illustrate the impact of online communities, social media trends, and humorous narratives in shaping the cryptocurrency landscape. As these coins continue to evolve, their communities play a significant role in their success, often driving both the hype and volatility associated with meme coins.

The Influence of Community-Driven Narratives and Social Media Memes

In the world of meme coins, community-driven narratives and social media memes play a paramount role in shaping the landscape and driving the popularity of these cryptocurrencies. Unlike traditional cryptocurrencies, which are primarily driven by technical specifications and underlying technology, meme coins thrive on the power of collective narratives and viral trends.

Online communities gather around these meme coins, creating a sense of belonging and shared enthusiasm. They actively contribute to discussions, promotions, and the creation of humorous narratives that capture the attention of social media users. This engagement not only fuels the visibility of meme coins but also drives their popularity and, at times, their volatility.

The influence of community-driven narratives and social media memes cannot be underestimated. They have the ability to propel a meme coin from obscurity to mainstream consciousness, attracting new investors and increasing trading volumes. Memes and online trends can quickly spread, creating a buzz around a particular coin and driving its value upwards.

However, it is crucial to recognize that the influence of community-driven narratives and social media memes also introduces risks. The hype surrounding meme coins can lead to sudden price fluctuations and increased market speculation. Investors should exercise caution and conduct thorough research before engaging in meme coin investments, as the influence of community sentiment and social media trends can be unpredictable.

In summary, the influence of community-driven narratives and social media memes is a defining characteristic of meme coins. These narratives and trends have the power to shape the perception and value of these cryptocurrencies, attracting both enthusiastic supporters and speculative investors. Understanding the dynamics of community-driven narratives and their impact on meme coins is essential for navigating this unique and evolving sector of the cryptocurrency market.

History of Meme Coins

Meme coins, with their playful and often humorous origins, have gained significant attention in the cryptocurrency space. These unique digital assets emerged as an entertaining spin-off from traditional cryptocurrencies, driven by online humor and the power of viral content. Here's a closer look at the key milestones and evolution of meme coins:

- Early Days and Online Humor: Meme coins began to gain traction as online communities embraced the idea of creating cryptocurrencies based on popular memes. The Dogecoin, launched in 2013 as a lighthearted joke, became a prominent early example of a meme coin. Its success sparked the imagination of creators and enthusiasts, leading to the birth of numerous other meme coins.

- Influencer Mentions and Popularity: The rise of social media and influential figures further contributed to the popularity of meme coins. As memes and viral content spread across platforms, popular influencers and celebrities started mentioning and endorsing these cryptocurrencies, attracting attention from a broader audience. This exposure helped meme coins gain momentum and wider acceptance.

- Key Milestones and Success Stories: Over time, meme coins achieved significant milestones and success stories. Memetic, cultural, and societal references continued to inspire the creation of new meme coins, each with its unique community and narrative. Some meme coins witnessed impressive price surges and became the center of attention within the cryptocurrency market, further fueling the interest in this distinctive sector.

The history of meme coins is a testament to the power of humor, viral content, and the community-driven nature of cryptocurrency. As the narrative surrounding meme coins continues to evolve, understanding their history provides valuable insights into their cultural relevance, market dynamics, and the opportunities they present.

Evolution and Key Milestones

The evolution of meme coins has been nothing short of remarkable, driven by viral trends and the power of online communities. These unique digital assets gained traction through their association with internet humor, which tapped into the collective imagination and humor of the masses. As people embraced and shared memes on social media platforms, certain cryptocurrencies emerged as symbols of these viral sensations.

One key milestone in the history of meme coins was the birth of Dogecoin in 2013. Inspired by the "Doge" meme featuring a Shiba Inu dog, Dogecoin quickly gained popularity for its lighthearted and playful nature. The coin's community-driven approach and philanthropic initiatives further solidified its position as a prominent meme coin.

Another significant milestone came in 2021, with the rise and subsequent explosion of interest in meme coins like SafeMoon and Shiba Inu. These coins captured the attention of investors and the general public alike, fueled by social media buzz and the endorsement of influential figures. This surge in popularity brought meme coins into the mainstream and sparked a wave of enthusiasm and curiosity within the cryptocurrency market.

The history of meme coins is a testament to the power of humor, viral content, and the community-driven nature of cryptocurrency. Understanding the evolution and key milestones of these unique digital assets provides valuable insights into their cultural relevance, market dynamics, and the opportunities they present.

Meme coins have carved a unique niche in the cryptocurrency market, primarily fueled by online humor and the influential power of social media influencers. These digital assets gained traction through their distinctive appeal, often originating from viral memes and internet culture. What started as playful experiments soon turned into a phenomenon, capturing the attention and imagination of a wide range of investors. The lighthearted nature and humorous branding of meme coins attracted a devoted online community who saw them as more than just financial investments—they were a way to participate in a cultural movement.

One of the key drivers of meme coin popularity is the influence of social media influencers. These individuals with large online followings have the ability to reach a massive audience, creating buzz and excitement around specific meme coins through their endorsements and mentions. When popular influencers publicly express their support or enthusiasm for a meme coin, it often leads to a surge in interest and investment, as their followers trust their judgment and want to join in on the fun.

Moreover, the viral nature of meme coins on social media platforms fuels their growth. Memes have the power to spread rapidly, captivating the attention of online communities and sparking conversations. As memes related to a specific coin gain traction, they generate curiosity and intrigue, attracting new investors who want to be part of the trend. This viral cycle of humor, online engagement, and influencer involvement has proven to be a potent formula in driving the popularity and success of meme coins in the cryptocurrency market.

However, it's important to note that while humor and online presence play a significant role in the initial traction of meme coins, investors should exercise caution and consider the inherent risks associated with these assets. The volatile nature of meme coins and the ever-changing sentiment within the online community can lead to unpredictable market behavior. Therefore, it's crucial to conduct thorough research, understand the underlying fundamentals, and approach meme coins with a balanced perspective.

Meme Coins vs. Traditional Cryptocurrencies

Meme coins and traditional cryptocurrencies differ in various aspects, ranging from their purpose and technology to community involvement. Understanding these differences is crucial for investors seeking to navigate the cryptocurrency market effectively.

Differences in Purpose, Technology, and Community Involvement

Meme coins often emerge as a playful or satirical take on traditional cryptocurrencies, aiming to capture the attention and enthusiasm of a specific online community. While traditional cryptocurrencies like Bitcoin and Ethereum serve as digital currencies or platforms for decentralized applications, meme coins typically lack a clear use case beyond their entertainment value.

In terms of technology, meme coins often piggyback on existing blockchain networks, leveraging the infrastructure and security provided by established cryptocurrencies. This allows meme coins to be created and traded relatively easily, with new projects frequently emerging. In contrast, traditional cryptocurrencies are built on their own dedicated blockchain networks, offering distinct features and functionalities.

Community involvement plays a significant role in the success of meme coins. These coins thrive on social engagement and foster dedicated fan-based communities that drive their popularity. The community's trust, transparency, and active communication are crucial factors contributing to the success or failure of meme coins. Traditional cryptocurrencies, while still benefiting from community support, tend to have a more diverse and widespread user base due to their broader range of applications.

By understanding the differences between meme coins and traditional cryptocurrencies, investors can make informed decisions and navigate the cryptocurrency landscape with a balanced perspective.

The Importance of Sentiment and Hype over Traditional Fundamentals

In the world of meme coins, sentiment and hype often take center stage, overshadowing traditional fundamentals typically considered in the realm of traditional investments. Unlike traditional cryptocurrencies that are evaluated based on factors like technology, utility, and market adoption, meme coins thrive on the power of collective enthusiasm and social media frenzy. The rise of meme coins is largely fueled by online communities that rally behind them, driven by the excitement and potential for quick gains.

While traditional fundamentals may take a backseat, it's essential to recognize that sentiment and hype can greatly influence the short-term performance of meme coins. The viral nature of these cryptocurrencies often sparks waves of speculative trading, creating volatile market dynamics. Investors must carefully navigate this landscape, understanding the role of sentiment and hype in driving price movements and making informed decisions that align with their risk tolerance and investment goals.

It's important to note that the hype surrounding meme coins can be short-lived and highly unpredictable. As such, investors should exercise caution and conduct thorough research before engaging in meme coin investments. While sentiment and hype may propel meme coins to new heights, it's crucial to maintain a balanced perspective and consider long-term sustainability and value creation when evaluating investment opportunities in the cryptocurrency market.

The Role of Community in Meme Coins

Meme coins thrive on the power of community engagement and fan-based interactions. The significance of social engagement cannot be overstated, as it plays a crucial role in the success of meme coins. These communities often foster trust, transparency, and open communication among their members, creating a sense of camaraderie and shared purpose. Investors and enthusiasts actively participate in discussions, sharing insights, and collectively driving the adoption and popularity of meme coins. The strength of these communities lies in their ability to build a loyal and dedicated following, which can contribute to the long-term sustainability and value creation of meme coins.

Market Dynamics of Meme Coins

Meme coins are known for their inherent volatility, characterized by rapid price fluctuations and often influenced by market sentiment and short-term trends. Liquidity, or the ease with which meme coins can be bought or sold, is a crucial factor that impacts their market dynamics. Understanding the trading patterns and market behavior of meme coins is essential for investors to make informed decisions. Additionally, the narrative surrounding meme coins can quickly shift, heavily influenced by social media trends and "meta" factors. Staying abreast of these narrative shifts can help investors navigate the ever-changing landscape of meme coins and respond to market dynamics effectively.

Volatility, liquidity, and trading patterns

Meme coins are often characterized by their high volatility, which refers to their tendency to experience rapid price fluctuations within short periods. The volatile nature of meme coins can present both opportunities and risks for investors. While sudden price surges can lead to significant gains, they can also result in substantial losses. It is crucial for investors to carefully analyze and understand the factors driving volatility in meme coins, including market sentiment, speculation, and external events impacting the broader cryptocurrency market.

In addition to volatility, liquidity is another important aspect to consider. Liquidity refers to the ease with which meme coins can be bought or sold without significantly impacting their price. Highly liquid meme coins tend to have large trading volumes and tight bid-ask spreads, allowing investors to enter and exit positions more efficiently. On the other hand, low liquidity can make it challenging to execute trades at desired prices, leading to potential slippage and increased transaction costs.

Understanding the trading patterns of meme coins is also crucial for investors. Technical analysis techniques, such as chart patterns and indicators, can provide insights into historical price movements and help identify potential trends. It is important to note that trading patterns in meme coins can be influenced by a wide range of factors, including social media trends, celebrity endorsements, and market sentiment. Staying informed about these patterns and market behavior can enable investors to make more informed trading decisions and potentially capitalize on short-term fluctuations.

Narrative shifts and "meta" trends influencing short-term market behavior

Meme coins are heavily influenced by narrative shifts and "meta" trends that emerge from social media platforms and online communities. The perception and popularity of meme coins can quickly change based on viral trends, cultural references, and community sentiment. Investors should closely monitor the evolving narratives surrounding meme coins, as they can significantly impact short-term market behavior.

For example, a meme coin that gains traction due to a popular social media campaign or celebrity endorsement might experience a surge in demand and price. Conversely, negative narratives or controversies surrounding a meme coin can lead to a sharp decline in its value. Investors need to be aware of these narrative shifts and distinguish between short-term hype and long-term value when making investment decisions.

To navigate the dynamic landscape of meme coins, investors should stay attuned to the latest social media trends, monitor community discussions, and conduct thorough research. By understanding narrative shifts and "meta" trends, investors can better gauge short-term market behavior and make informed decisions based on a comprehensive understanding of the meme coin's underlying fundamentals and potential for long-term growth.

Legal and Regulatory Considerations

When it comes to investing in meme coins, understanding global regulations and compliance issues is essential to protect investors and ensure a fair and transparent market. Different countries have varying legal frameworks that govern digital currencies, and staying informed about these regulations can help investors navigate the evolving landscape. Familiarizing oneself with best practices for staying within the law, such as know-your-customer (KYC) and anti-money laundering (AML) requirements, can contribute to a safer and more compliant investment experience.

Ethical Considerations

Investing in meme coins also requires careful attention to ethical considerations. Given the speculative nature of meme coins and the potential for scams and fraudulent activities, it is crucial to exercise caution and conduct thorough research before investing. Avoiding investments in projects that lack transparency or engage in misleading practices is essential. It is important to prioritize honest communication, ethical promotion, and responsible investment practices to uphold the integrity of the market and protect investors' interests.

Potential Risks and Rewards

Investing in meme coins involves navigating a landscape characterized by high volatility and trading patterns. While the potential for high returns exists, investors must balance this with the inherent risks. Understanding the dynamics of meme coins' price movements, liquidity, and trading patterns can help investors make informed decisions. It is important to recognize when to capitalize on "hot" narratives while also exercising caution and not succumbing to FOMO (fear of missing out). Risk management strategies, diversification, and setting realistic investment goals can aid in mitigating risks and optimizing potential rewards.

Future Trends in Meme Coins and Cryptocurrency

As the world of cryptocurrencies continues to evolve, meme coins have emerged as a captivating trend, capturing the attention of investors and enthusiasts alike. Looking ahead, several exciting developments and patterns are shaping the future of meme coins and the broader cryptocurrency landscape. Here are some key trends to watch:

- **Emerging Patterns and Potential Developments**: Meme coins are likely to witness further experimentation and innovation in their tokenomics and overall design. Developers and communities are exploring ways to strike a balance between fun and sustainable value creation, fueling the rise of new meme coin projects with unique features and utility.

- **The Growing Role of Blockchain Analytics**: With the increasing popularity of meme coins, the importance of blockchain analytics tools is becoming more evident. These tools provide valuable insights into market trends, transaction patterns, and the behavior of meme coin communities. Leveraging blockchain analytics enables investors and project teams to make more informed decisions and identify opportunities in this dynamic space.

- **AI-Driven Tools and Integrated Trading Platforms**: As meme coins continue to gain traction, the integration of artificial intelligence (AI) tools into trading platforms is likely to increase. AI-driven algorithms can help investors analyze market data, detect patterns, and make data-driven investment decisions. Furthermore, integrated trading platforms that offer seamless access to various meme coins and traditional cryptocurrencies are expected to emerge, providing users with convenience and broader investment opportunities.

By keeping an eye on these trends, meme coin enthusiasts and investors can stay ahead of the curve and navigate the rapidly evolving landscape of cryptocurrency. As the meme coin phenomenon evolves, it is essential to embrace innovation while also exercising caution and staying informed about market developments.

Chapter 2
Planning and Conceptualizing Your Meme Coin

In this chapter, we delve into the crucial process of planning and conceptualizing your meme coin. As the meme coin phenomenon continues to captivate the cryptocurrency world, it is essential to lay a solid foundation for your coin's success. We will explore key considerations such as defining your coin's purpose and vision, identifying your target audience, and developing a unique selling proposition (USP). Additionally, we will delve into the intricacies of tokenomics design, including supply, distribution, incentives, and the importance of on-chain verifiable token dynamics. By understanding and implementing these essential elements, you can set your meme coin on the path to stand out in the competitive crypto landscape and capture the attention of investors and enthusiasts alike. So, let's embark on this exciting journey of planning and conceptualizing your meme coin!

Defining Your Coin's Purpose and Vision

Defining a clear purpose and vision for your meme coin is crucial for its success and long-term sustainability. It involves articulating the fundamental goals and objectives that your coin aims to achieve in the crypto landscape. Here are some key considerations to help you define your coin's purpose and vision:

1. **Identify a Problem or Need**: Start by identifying a specific problem

or need within the crypto community that your meme coin can address. This could be related to transparency, accessibility, community engagement, or any other area where you believe there is room for improvement.

2. **Craft a Compelling Value Proposition**: Determine what makes your meme coin unique and how it adds value to the crypto ecosystem. What sets it apart from other meme coins? Is there a particular aspect of your coin's design, functionality, or community that makes it stand out? Articulate your value proposition clearly to attract and engage potential investors and supporters.

3. **Establish Clear Goals**: Define the short-term and long-term goals you want to achieve with your meme coin. These goals could include growing a vibrant and engaged community, listing on major exchanges, or becoming a recognized name in the meme coin space. Having well-defined goals will guide your decision-making and help you measure your progress.

4. **Align Your Coin's Purpose with Your Target Audience**: Consider who your target audience is and what they value in a meme coin. Align your coin's purpose and vision with the needs and expectations of your intended audience. This will help you attract the right supporters and build a strong community around your coin.

5. **Communicate Your Vision Effectively**: Clearly communicate your coin's purpose and vision through your branding, messaging, and marketing efforts. Develop a compelling narrative that resonates with your target audience and inspires them to become part of your coin's journey.

By defining your coin's purpose and vision, you lay the foundation for a compelling and meaningful meme coin that can capture the attention and support of the crypto community.

Setting Clear Objectives and Market Positioning

Setting clear objectives and defining a strong market positioning is essential for the success of your coin. Clearly articulate your short-term and long-term goals, whether it's creating a decentralized ecosystem, fostering community engagement, or supporting a specific cause. Having well-defined objectives allows you to align your efforts and resources towards achieving them.

Market positioning involves identifying your unique value proposition and understanding how you differentiate yourself from other meme coins in the market. Consider what makes your coin stand out - whether it's through branding, narrative, or innovative tokenomics. Communicate these unique selling points effectively to attract and engage your target audience.

By setting clear objectives and establishing a distinct market positioning, you can create a strong foundation for your meme coin's success in the competitive crypto landscape. Stay focused, adapt as needed, and continue to refine your strategy to capture the interest and support of the crypto community.

Identifying Your Target Audience

To ensure the success of your meme coin, it is crucial to have a clear understanding of your target audience and their online behavior. Identifying the right audience will enable you to tailor your marketing efforts and effectively engage with those who are most likely to support your coin. Here are some key steps to help you in this process:

1. **Research and Analysis**: Conduct thorough research to gain insights into the crypto community and its various segments. Analyze existing meme coin enthusiasts, their demographics, interests, and online habits. This will help you create personas that represent your ideal

target audience.

2. **Community Engagement**: Actively engage with the crypto community through social media platforms, forums, and online communities. Participate in discussions, ask questions, and listen to their needs and preferences. This will help you gain a deeper understanding of their motivations and expectations.

3. **Data Analysis**: Utilize analytics tools and platforms to gather data on user engagement, website traffic, and social media interactions. Analyzing this data will provide valuable insights into the demographic profile, online behavior, and preferences of your existing audience.

4. **Surveys and Feedback**: Conduct surveys or collect feedback from your existing community to gather specific information about their interests, expectations, and motivations for supporting meme coins. This feedback will help you refine your marketing strategy and tailor your messaging to resonate with your target audience.

By understanding who will support your meme coin and their online behavior, you can develop targeted marketing campaigns, create engaging content, and foster meaningful connections with your audience. Remember, a deep understanding of your target audience will set the foundation for the success of your meme coin in the competitive crypto landscape.

Understanding Who Will Support Your Coin and Their Online Behavior

Understanding who will support your coin and their online behavior is crucial for the success of your meme coin in the competitive crypto landscape. Identifying your target audience allows you to tailor your marketing strategies, develop engaging content, and foster meaningful connections. Consider the following aspects when understanding your audience:

• **Demographics**: Analyze the demographic characteristics of your target audience, such as age, gender, location, and occupation. This information helps you customize your messaging and target your marketing efforts more effectively.

- **Online Behavior**: Gain insights into the online behavior of your audience. Identify the platforms they frequent, the communities they engage with, and their preferred communication channels. This knowledge enables you to reach them in the right place and at the right time, maximizing the impact of your marketing campaigns.

- **Interests and Preferences**: Understand the interests, preferences, and values of your target audience. This knowledge helps you develop content that resonates with them, creating a sense of connection and community around your meme coin.

- **Motivations and Goals**: Dive deeper into the motivations and goals of your audience when it comes to cryptocurrency investments. Are they seeking financial gains, supporting a cause, or simply looking for entertainment? Understanding their motivations allows you to align your coin's value proposition with their desires, increasing the likelihood of attracting their support.

By gaining a deep understanding of your target audience, you can optimize your marketing strategies, create meaningful engagement, and ultimately build a strong and loyal community around your meme coin.

Unique Selling Proposition (USP)

A unique selling proposition (USP) is the distinctive quality or feature that sets your meme coin apart from others in the market. It is the value proposition that captures the attention and interest of potential investors and community members. To establish a strong USP for your meme coin, you need to differentiate it through branding, narrative, or innovative tokenomics. This can be achieved by crafting a compelling story that resonates with your target audience, highlighting

the unique benefits and value that your coin brings to the market. By effectively communicating your USP, you can attract supporters who align with your coin's vision and values, fostering trust and loyalty within your community.

When it comes to differentiating your meme coin through branding, narrative, or innovative tokenomics, leveraging examples can help illustrate the possibilities and inspire your approach. Let's explore how you can achieve this:

Tokenomics: Designing the Economic Model

Look at successful meme coins like Dogecoin, which gained traction by adopting a unique tokenomics model with a large supply and a low transaction cost. This design created a sense of accessibility and encouraged widespread participation.

Choosing the Right Blockchain Platform

Consider the case of SafeMoon, which gained popularity by launching on the Binance Smart Chain. Leveraging the BNB Chain allowed for faster transactions and lower fees, attracting investors looking for efficiency and cost-effectiveness.

Naming and Branding Your Meme Coin

Take inspiration from coins like Shiba Inu, which drew attention by aligning its name and brand with popular narratives and internet trends. Creating a memorable and relatable identity can help your coin stand out and resonate with your target audience.

Developing a Roadmap

Examine the roadmap of meme coins like Baby Doge Coin, which outlined clear objectives and milestones. A well-defined roadmap demonstrates your commitment to the project and provides a sense of direction, instilling confidence in your community and investors.

By studying the success stories and approaches of prominent meme coins, you can gain valuable insights and inspiration to differentiate your coin. Remember, the key is to craft a compelling story, embrace innovative tokenomics, and build a strong brand that captures the attention and imagination of your target audience.

Differentiating through Branding, Narrative, or Innovative Tokenomics

In the world of meme coins, creating a unique and captivating presence is essential for standing out from the crowd. One effective approach is to differentiate your coin through branding, narrative, or innovative tokenomics. By developing a compelling brand identity, crafting a captivating story, and implementing innovative tokenomic features, you can capture the attention and imagination of your target audience. Let's explore each of these strategies in more detail:

Branding: Creating a memorable brand identity is crucial for attracting and retaining supporters. Consider developing a distinct visual identity, including a unique logo, color scheme, and visual assets that resonate with your target audience. It's also essential to align your brand messaging with popular narratives or themes to create a strong connection with your community.

Narrative: A compelling narrative can help your meme coin gain traction and build a dedicated following. Craft a story that resonates with your target audience and emphasizes the value proposition of your coin. Whether it's supporting a cause, challenging the status quo, or providing a form of entertainment, a well-crafted narrative can create a sense of community and purpose around your coin.

Innovative Tokenomics: Designing innovative tokenomic features can set your meme coin apart from others in the market. Consider exploring unique mechanisms for supply, distribution, incentives, and fair launches. Transparency is key, so ensure that your token dynamics are verifiable on-chain, providing a clear understanding of how your coin operates.

By strategically differentiating your meme coin through branding, narrative, or innovative tokenomics, you can position yourself for success in the competitive landscape of meme coins. Remember to continuously adapt and evolve your strategies to stay relevant and capture the interest of your ever-changing audience.

Tokenomics: Designing the Economic Model

Tokenomics is a crucial aspect of creating a successful meme coin. It involves designing the economic model that governs the supply, distribution, incentives, and launch strategies of your coin. By carefully considering these factors, you can create an ecosystem that fosters sustainability, value appreciation, and community engagement. Here are key considerations when designing the economic model for your meme coin:

- **Supply and Distribution**: Determine the total supply of your coin and plan its distribution. Consider factors like token burns, staking mechanisms, and lock-up periods to control the circulating supply and ensure a balanced distribution.

- **Incentives**: Design incentive structures to encourage participation and engagement within your community. This can include rewards for holding and staking tokens, providing liquidity, or participating in governance processes.

- **Fair Launches**: Choose an appropriate launch strategy that ensures fairness and avoids favoritism. This can involve mechanisms like whitelisting, initial liquidity locks, or time-based releases to gradually introduce your coin to the market.

- **Transparency**: Ensure that your token dynamics are verifiable on-chain, providing a clear understanding of how your coin operates. Transparency builds trust among your community and reinforces confidence in the long-term viability of your meme coin.

By carefully considering these aspects of tokenomics, you can create an economic model that aligns with your goals and enhances the value proposition of your meme coin.

Supply, Distribution, Incentives, and Fair Launches

When creating a meme coin, it is essential to carefully consider aspects related to supply, distribution, incentives, and fair launches. These factors play a crucial role in shaping the dynamics of your coin and can greatly impact its long-term success. Here's a closer look at each of these aspects:

- **Supply**: Determining the total supply of your meme coin is a critical decision. It should be based on various considerations such as market demand, token utility, and long-term sustainability. Careful supply management can help maintain scarcity and ensure a healthy balance between available tokens and market demand.

- **Distribution**: Developing a well-thought-out distribution strategy is vital to ensure a fair and inclusive launch of your meme coin. Consider different methods such as initial coin offerings (ICOs), airdrops, or liquidity mining to distribute tokens among early participants and supporters. Fair distribution can help foster a strong community and promote wider adoption.

- **Incentives**: Designing an incentive structure is crucial for incentivizing desired behaviors within your community. This can include rewarding token holders, liquidity providers, or participants in governance and decision-making processes. Well-designed incentives can help drive user engagement, liquidity, and long-term growth.

- **Fair Launches**: Conducting a fair launch is key to building trust and credibility. It involves ensuring equal opportunities for all participants to acquire tokens at the initial stages. Fair launches can be achieved through mechanisms such as decentralized auctions, limit orders, or token swaps, allowing for a transparent and equitable distribution of tokens.

By carefully considering and implementing these aspects of supply, distribution, incentives, and fair launches, you can create a solid foundation for the success and sustainability of your meme coin, fostering trust, engagement, and long-term growth within your community.

Ensuring Transparency Through On-chain Verifiable Token Dynamics

Ensuring transparency through on-chain verifiable token dynamics is crucial for building trust and confidence among investors and community members. By leveraging blockchain technology, you can establish a robust system that allows stakeholders to verify the authenticity and accuracy of token transactions and holdings. Implementing on-chain verifiability provides transparency in several key areas:

Transaction Visibility: On-chain verifiable token dynamics enable individuals to track and verify token transactions in real-time. This transparency allows for a comprehensive audit trail, ensuring that all transactions are recorded and accessible to the public.

Token Supply and Distribution: By utilizing blockchain technology, you can provide a transparent view of the token supply and distribution. This includes details such as the initial token allocation, token sales, and any subsequent token minting or burning events. Stakeholders can verify the legitimacy and fairness of the token distribution process.

Token Ownership: On-chain verifiability allows individuals to verify token ownership and holdings. This ensures that the token supply is accurately represented and prevents fraudulent activities, such as double-spending or unauthorized token transfers.

Smart Contract Audits: Conducting smart contract audits and making the results publicly available enhances transparency and provides assurance to investors and community members. Audits help identify and resolve potential vulnerabilities or weaknesses in the smart contract code, ensuring the security and integrity of the token ecosystem.

By incorporating on-chain verifiable token dynamics, you establish a transparent and accountable framework that fosters trust and confidence within your community. This transparency not only attracts investors but also cultivates an engaged and informed community that is essential for the long-term success and sustainability of your meme coin.

Choosing the Right Blockchain Platform

When it comes to creating a successful meme coin, choosing the right blockchain platform is crucial. Ethereum, BNB Chain, Polygon, and Solana are among the top choices known for their robust infrastructure and capabilities. These platforms offer enhanced traceability and verification, ensuring the integrity and transparency of your token ecosystem. Here's a closer look at each platform:

1. **Ethereum**: As one of the most popular blockchain platforms, Ethereum provides a solid foundation for meme coins. It offers smart contract functionality and a vast ecosystem of decentralized applications (dApps), making it a trusted choice for developers and investors alike.

2. **BNB Chain**: Built by Binance, BNB Chain presents a fast and efficient blockchain platform for meme coins. It offers low transaction fees and seamless integration with Binance's ecosystem, providing access to a large and active community.

3. **Polygon**: Formerly known as Matic Network, Polygon aims to solve scalability issues on Ethereum. It offers a layer 2 solution that enhances the speed and efficiency of transactions, making it an attractive option for meme coin projects looking for quick and cost-effective transactions.

4. **Solana**: Solana is a high-performance blockchain platform known for its scalability and low transaction costs. It boasts fast transaction speeds and high throughput, making it suitable for meme coins that require quick execution and high-volume transactions.

Carefully evaluating the features, scalability, community support, and ecosystem of each platform will help you make an informed decision that aligns with your project's specific needs for enhanced traceability and verification.

Naming and Branding Your Meme Coin

Creating a memorable identity aligned with popular narratives is a crucial step in developing your meme coin. The name and branding of your coin play a significant role in attracting attention and building a strong community around it. Consider the following tips as you embark on this creative process:

- **Reflect the Narrative**: Choose a name and brand that align with the theme or concept behind your meme coin. It should resonate with your target audience and capture the essence of your project's vision.

- **Capture Attention**: Aim for a catchy and memorable name that stands out in the crowded cryptocurrency market. Make sure it captures the essence of your coin's purpose while being unique and identifiable.

- **Tell a Story**: Develop a compelling narrative around your meme coin that sparks curiosity and engagement. Craft a backstory or mythology that captures the imagination of potential investors and community members.

- **Visual Appeal**: Create a visually appealing logo and design elements that align with your brand identity. Consider employing graphic designers or leveraging online design tools to ensure a professional and eye-catching visual representation.

- **Consistency and Authenticity**: Ensure consistency in your branding across different channels, including social media, websites, and marketing materials. Stay true to your brand values and maintain an authentic voice that resonates with your community.

Remember, the name and branding of your meme coin will be the first impression for potential investors and community members. Take the time to brainstorm, gather feedback, and refine your brand identity to create a lasting and impactful presence in the world of meme coins.

Developing a Roadmap

Setting a well-defined roadmap is crucial for the success of your meme coin project. It provides a clear direction and helps you stay focused on your goals. When developing your roadmap, consider setting both short-term and long-term milestones with flexibility to adapt to market shifts. This allows you to navigate the ever-changing landscape of meme coins and adjust your strategies accordingly. By outlining specific targets and timelines, you can track your progress, measure achievements, and communicate your vision to potential investors and community members. Remember, a well-crafted roadmap serves as a roadmap to success, guiding your project towards its ultimate objectives.

Building a Team: Assembling Developers, Marketers, and Community Managers

One of the crucial steps in creating and launching your meme coin is building a talented and dedicated team. Assemble a team of skilled developers, marketers, and community managers who share your vision and can contribute their expertise to the project. Developers will play a key role in coding and implementing the technical aspects of your meme coin. Marketers will help in promoting and spreading awareness about your coin, while community managers will engage with potential investors and foster a vibrant community around your project.

Additionally, consider leveraging community "alpha" groups for valuable insights. These groups can provide feedback, suggestions, and early testing of your meme coin, allowing you to refine and improve your project based on real-world input. By building a strong and collaborative team, you can harness the collective knowledge and skills needed to navigate the dynamic world of meme coins and set your project on a path to success.

Budgeting and Funding

When creating your meme coin, it is crucial to have a clear understanding of your budget and funding requirements. Estimating the costs associated with developing, launching, and promoting your project is essential for effective financial planning. This includes expenses related to smart contract development, marketing, community management, and any other necessary resources. By accurately estimating your costs, you can ensure that you have the necessary funds available to support your project's success.

In addition to estimating costs, considering strategic partnerships with tooling platforms can provide valuable support and resources for your meme coin project. Collaborating with established platforms that specialize in meme coins and blockchain technology can offer access to tools, services, and expertise that can enhance your project's development and growth. These partnerships can provide you with access to a wider audience, additional funding opportunities, and valuable industry insights.

By carefully budgeting and exploring strategic partnerships with tooling platforms, you can position your meme coin project for success, ensuring that you have the necessary financial resources and support to bring your vision to life.

In conclusion, chapter 2 has provided valuable insights into the critical aspects of financial planning and legal structuring for your meme coin project. By carefully budgeting and establishing strategic partnerships, you can position your project for success, gaining access to a wider audience, additional funding opportunities, and industry insights. Furthermore, setting a solid legal framework ensures trust and legitimacy, essential for the long-term viability of your project. With these foundational elements in place, you are well-prepared to embark on the exciting journey of creating your meme coin in the next chapter. Stay tuned for an exploration of the technical requirements and considerations that will bring your vision to life.

Chapter 3
Creating Your Meme Coin

In this chapter, we explore the essential steps and considerations for creating your meme coin. We start by discussing the technical requirements and prerequisites, emphasizing the importance of having coding skills or hiring a developer. Additionally, we delve into the selection of blockchain tools for verifying contract integrity, such as audits, to ensure the security and reliability of your smart contracts. We also highlight the significance of clean code for easy on-chain verification.

Next, we guide you through the process of choosing token standards, including ERC-20, BEP-20, and SPL (Solana), which promote interoperability and increase market acceptance of your meme coin. Lastly, we emphasize the importance of testing your smart contract to ensure its security and functionality.

By following these guidelines and best practices, you can navigate the technical aspects of creating your meme coin and lay a solid foundation for success in the booming world of cryptocurrency.

Technical Requirements and Prerequisites

To embark on the journey of creating your meme coin, there are certain technical requirements and prerequisites that you need to consider. Whether you possess coding skills or plan to hire a developer, having a solid understanding of the technical aspects is crucial for success in the world of cryptocurrency.

Necessary Coding Skills or Hiring a Developer

Creating a meme coin requires a certain level of coding expertise. If you have the necessary skills, you can take on the task yourself. However, if coding is not your forte, it is advisable to hire a developer who specializes in smart contract development and blockchain technology. A skilled developer can ensure the security and functionality of your smart contract, saving you time and effort.

Choosing Blockchain Tools for Verifying Contract Integrity (e.g., Audits)

When developing a meme coin, it is essential to ensure the integrity of your smart contract. This involves verifying its security and functionality. One way to achieve this is by utilizing blockchain tools and services that offer audits and verification services. These tools can help identify potential vulnerabilities or issues in your smart contract, allowing you to address them before deployment.

Smart Contract Development

Writing and deploying a secure smart contract is a critical step in creating your meme coin. A well-written smart contract is essential for ensuring the proper functioning of your coin and safeguarding it against potential security risks. It is important to follow best practices and adopt security measures to mitigate the chances of vulnerabilities or exploits.

Choosing Token Standards

When creating a meme coin, you need to choose the appropriate token standard that aligns with your goals. The most common token standards are ERC-20 (Ethereum), BEP-20 (Binance Smart Chain), and SPL (Solana). Selecting the right token standard ensures interoperability with existing platforms and increases market acceptance for your meme coin.

Remember, investing time and effort in understanding the technical requirements and prerequisites of creating your meme coin will provide a solid foundation for its success. By following best practices, conducting thorough testing, and incorporating specialized verification tools, you can ensure the security, functionality, and market acceptance of your meme coin.

Introducing Pump.fun: Creating Meme Coins Made Easy

If you're looking for a platform that simplifies the process of creating meme coins, look no further than Pump.fun. This innovative platform provides a user-friendly interface and a comprehensive set of tools to bring your meme coin ideas to life. With Pump.fun, you can unleash your creativity and tap into the booming world of meme coins with ease. Let's dive into how you can leverage this platform to create your very own meme coin and join the exciting wave of digital assets.

Choosing Token Standards with Pump.fun

When utilizing Pump.fun to create your very own meme coin, you have the flexibility to choose from different token standards to ensure interoperability and market acceptance. Here's a step-by-step guide on how to choose the token standards using Pump.fun:

1. **Visit Pump.fun**: Head to the Pump.fun website and navigate to the token creation section.

2. **Token Standards**: Explore the available token standards, including ERC-20 (Ethereum), BEP-20 (Binance Smart Chain), and SPL (Solana).

Consider the features, compatibility, and advantages of each standard to select the one that best suits your project's goals and target audience.

3. **Research and Analysis**: Conduct thorough research on each token standard, considering factors such as the existing ecosystem, community support, and developer resources. Evaluate their track records and the level of adoption in the market to make an informed decision.

4. **Interoperability and Market Acceptance**: Assess the interoperability of the token standard you choose, ensuring that it can seamlessly integrate and interact with other platforms and exchanges. Consider the market acceptance and liquidity of tokens based on the chosen standard to maximize visibility and trading opportunities.

By carefully considering these steps and leveraging the options provided by Pump.fun, you can confidently select the token standard that aligns with your project's requirements, ensuring smooth interoperability and broad market acceptance for your meme coin.

Step By Step on Creating Your First Meme Coin

Below is a general, step-by-step walkthrough for creating your first meme coin using Pump.fun. Keep in mind that the exact steps or interface details may change over time, so always consult the official Pump.fun documentation or support channels for the most up-to-date instructions. Also remember that creating a token comes with responsibility—ensure you understand the technical and legal implications before proceeding.

Step 1: Prepare Your Digital Wallet

What's a Wallet?
A crypto wallet is like a digital version of a physical wallet. It stores your cryptocurrency and connects to websites that let you create or trade tokens.

How to Get One:

1. **Choose a Wallet Provider:** Popular options include MetaMask, Coinbase Wallet, or Trust Wallet. You'll need to install a browser extension or download an app.

2. **Create Your Wallet:** Follow the instructions provided by your chosen wallet service. You'll likely need to write down a "seed phrase" (a series of words) somewhere safe. This seed phrase is like the password to your wallet—never share it with anyone.

3. **Add Funds:** To create a token, you must pay transaction fees (known as "gas") in the blockchain's native currency. For example, on Ethereum you'll need some ETH. Buy or transfer a small amount into your new wallet so you can cover these costs.

Step 2: Visit Pump.fun

Go to the Website:

Open your browser and navigate to https://pump.fun/. This is the platform you'll use to create your meme coin. Make sure you're on the correct and official website.

Connect Your Wallet:

1. Look for a "Connect Wallet" or similar button on the Pump.fun homepage.

2. Click it and select your wallet provider (for example, MetaMask).

3. A window from your wallet should pop up asking you to confirm the connection. Approve the request so Pump.fun can interact with your wallet (this lets the site know which address you're using to create the token).

Step 3: Choose Your Blockchain Network

What's a Network?

A blockchain network is like a separate universe for tokens and transactions. Ethereum Mainnet, Polygon, and Arbitrum are examples of different networks. Each network has its own speed, transaction costs, and user base.

Selecting the Right Network:

- If you want a widely recognized environment (though often more expensive), choose Ethereum Mainnet.

- If you want cheaper and faster transactions, consider other networks like Polygon or Arbitrum.

On Pump.fun, select the network you prefer. Make sure your wallet is also set to that same network.

Step 4: Start the Token Creation Process

Find the "Create Token" Feature:

Look on the Pump.fun interface for a button or menu option that says something like "Create Token" or "Launch New Token." Click on it, and it should open up a form where you'll enter all the details about your meme coin.

Enter Your Token's Details:

- **Name:** Pick a unique, fun name related to your meme's theme. For example, if your meme is about dogs, a name like "WoofCoin" might fit.

- **Symbol:** This is a short abbreviation for your coin, often shown with a dollar sign. For example, if you named your coin WoofCoin, you might use "WOOF."

- **Total Supply:** Decide how many tokens you want to exist. Many meme coins have a huge supply—like billions or trillions—but it's completely up to you. Just remember that the more tokens you have, the less "rare" each token is.

Step 5: Adjusting Advanced Settings (Optional)

Depending on what Pump.fun offers, you might see extra options like adding special transaction fees, setting up liquidity pools, or other features. If you're a beginner, it's often best to keep things simple for your first try. You can always learn about advanced features later.

Step 6: Review the Contract and Confirm

What's a Contract?
Your meme coin will be managed by a piece of code called a "smart contract." This code handles how the token is created, who owns it, and how it's transferred.

Pump.fun usually handles the smart contract part for you. They'll provide a template that follows standard token rules (like ERC-20 on Ethereum). This helps ensure your token will be compatible with wallets and exchanges.

Reviewing and Confirming:

1. Look over the details you entered. Make sure the name, symbol, and supply are correct.

2. Check if there's an estimate of transaction fees (gas fees). You need to have enough funds in your wallet to cover this.

3. If everything looks good, click "Deploy" or "Create Token."

Your wallet will ask you to confirm the transaction. Double-check the costs and confirm it. Now, wait patiently for the blockchain to process your request. This can take a few seconds or a few minutes.

Step 7: Token Confirmation and Address

Once the transaction is confirmed, your meme coin's smart contract is officially live on the blockchain. Pump.fun will show you your new token's contract address. This address is like the unique fingerprint of your coin.

What to Do With the Contract Address:

1. Copy it and keep it somewhere safe.

2. Use it to add your token to your wallet so you can see it and manage it.

Step 8: Add Your Token to Your Wallet

Open your wallet and look for an "Add Token" or "Import Token" button. Paste in your token's contract address, and your wallet should automatically detect the name and symbol you set. Once added, you'll see your total supply of tokens right in your wallet.

Step 9: Distribute or Sell Your Tokens (Optional)

Just creating a token doesn't automatically make it tradable. If you want others to be able to buy or sell your meme coin, you may need to take extra steps:

- **Airdrops:** Send some tokens to friends, followers, or community members to spread the word.

- **Liquidity Pools:** If you want your token to be traded on decentralized exchanges (like Uniswap), you'll need to create a liquidity pool. This involves depositing a portion of your tokens along with some cryptocurrency (like ETH) so that people can swap freely.

Pump.fun may offer guidance or tools for this step. If not, you can use popular exchanges and follow their instructions to create a pool.

Step 10: Market Your Meme Coin

A meme coin thrives on community and hype. Spread the word through social media, create a fun storyline around your coin, and engage with people who find it interesting or amusing. Meme coins often gain value from the community's enthusiasm, so consider setting up a Twitter account, Discord server, or Telegram chat where fans can gather.

Creating a Whitepaper: Documenting Details, Vision, and Tokenomics for Transparency

A crucial step in launching a successful meme coin is creating a comprehensive whitepaper. The whitepaper serves as a guiding document that outlines the key details, vision, and tokenomics of your project, providing transparency to potential investors, community members, and stakeholders. It is an opportunity to establish credibility and showcase the uniqueness of your meme coin. The whitepaper should include essential information such as the project's goals, the problem it aims to solve, the team behind the project, the token distribution and allocation, the tokenomics, and the roadmap for future development. By clearly articulating these aspects, you not only provide transparency but also build trust with your audience, ensuring they have a clear understanding of your project's purpose and potential.

Designing Visual Assets: Memorable Logos, Websites, and Promotional Materials

After creating your meme coin and setting it up for potential community growth, it's time to focus on its "visual identity." This means designing the images, logos, and websites that people will see and associate with your coin. These visual assets help tell a story, build recognition, and convey the fun, memorable qualities of your meme coin. You don't have to be a professional designer to make something eye-catching—just follow a few simple guidelines and use the tools available to you.

Step 1: Start with a Concept or Theme

Why It Matters:

Your meme coin probably has a fun or unique idea behind it (like a cute dog character or a silly internet joke). Take that theme and use it as inspiration for your visuals. Think about what emotions or ideas you want people to feel when they see your designs.

Examples:

- If your token is inspired by a particular animal, use colors, shapes, or patterns that remind people of that animal's environment.

- If it's based on a joke, find a way to visually represent that humor.

Step 2: Create a Simple, Recognizable Logo

What Makes a Good Logo?:

- **Simplicity:** Avoid cramming too many details into your logo. It should look good as a small icon on social media or as a large image on a website.

- **Color Choice:** Pick colors that reflect the mood you want. Bright, cheerful colors might say "fun and playful," while darker tones might feel more serious or edgy.

- **Flexibility:** Your logo should look good in different formats. Test it against a white background, a dark background, and in various sizes.

Tools to Use:

- Free design programs like Canva or Photopea for beginners.

- Pre-made templates for basic shapes and fonts to save time.

Step 3: Design a User-Friendly Website

Why a Website?:
A website serves as a home base for your project. It's where people go to learn about your token, team, roadmap, and any special features or upcoming events.

Key Elements:

1. **Clear Navigation:** Make it easy for visitors to find what they need. Include simple menus with clear labels like "About," "Tokenomics," or "Roadmap."

2. **Visually Consistent:** Use the same colors, fonts, and overall style as your logo. This helps everything feel connected and professional.

3. **Mobile-Friendly:** Many people browse on their phones. Choose a website template (like those offered by Wix, Squarespace, or Word-Press) that automatically looks good on mobile devices.

Step 4: Promotional Materials to Spread the Word

What Are Promotional Materials?:
These can be social media posts, banners, infographics, short videos, or even GIFs. They help you tell your story, share news, and highlight what makes your meme coin special.

Ideas for Content:

- **Social Media Posts:** Show off fun artwork, announce giveaways, or introduce team members.

- **Short Videos or Memes:** A quick, funny clip can make your project more shareable.

- **Infographics:** Visual charts or graphs explaining your token's supply, roadmap, or community growth can help people understand your project at a glance.

Keep It Consistent:

Always use your core design elements—logo, color scheme, and font choices—to maintain a cohesive brand identity. When people see these visuals again and again, they'll start to recognize your meme coin instantly.

Step 5: Gather Feedback and Improve

Listen to Your Community:

Don't be afraid to share early drafts of your designs and ask for feedback. Your community might offer great suggestions for color changes, logo tweaks, or new promotional ideas.

Make Iterative Improvements:

Design is a process. As your meme coin grows, feel free to update your visuals to keep things fresh and aligned with your evolving brand.

Step 6: Stay Inspired and Have Fun

Where to Find Inspiration:

Browse other successful meme coins, check out popular brands, or look at trending memes. Take note of what stands out and think about how you can apply those ideas to your own designs.

Remember, It's All About Your Community:

Your visual identity helps attract attention and sets the tone for your project. Have fun with it, be creative, and never forget that these assets are a reflection of the playful, community-driven spirit of your meme coin.

Launching Your Meme Coin: Coordinating a Successful, Hype-Driven Launch with Verified Wallet Addresses

Creating your meme coin is only part of the journey. The next big step is launching it to the public in a way that excites your community, drives interest, and builds trust. This often involves setting a specific launch time, verifying wallet addresses for fairness, and creating a sense of excitement around your project's debut. Below are beginner-friendly steps to help you manage a smooth, hype-driven launch.

Step 1: Set a Clear Launch Date and Time

Why It Matters:
Having a specific launch date and time lets your community know exactly when they can start buying or interacting with your meme coin. This creates anticipation and helps everyone prepare.

How to Choose a Time:

- **Community Time Zones:** If most of your supporters are in a particular region, pick a time that's convenient for them.

- **Avoiding Busy Periods:** Steer clear of major holidays or events that might distract potential buyers.

Once you've chosen a date, announce it well in advance through social media, your website, and any community chats.

Step 2: Verify Wallet Addresses for Fair Participation

What Are Verified Wallet Addresses?:
A verified wallet address is one you've pre-approved or recognized as valid before the token launch. By verifying addresses, you can reduce scams, ensure your community members get priority, and build trust by being transparent about who's involved.

How to Verify Addresses:

1. **Collect Addresses Early:** Ask interested community members to submit their wallet addresses through a secure form on your website or a trusted platform.

2. **Create a Whitelist:** Make a list of these addresses and keep it handy. This list is often called a "whitelist."

3. **Share the List:** Before launch, show the community which addresses are included so everyone knows who gets early access or special privileges.

This approach helps loyal supporters secure their tokens and prevents unknown parties from dominating the launch.

Step 3: Communicate Launch Details Clearly

Why Communication Is Key:
Your community needs to know how and where to get your token at launch. Provide step-by-step instructions so even beginners can participate easily.

What to Include:

- **Where to Buy:** If you're launching on a decentralized exchange, share the exact link.

- **When to Buy:** Remind everyone of the launch time and any time zone conversions.

- **How Much to Prepare:** Suggest how much of the network's native currency (e.g., ETH) they should have for buying your token and covering transaction fees.

Put this information on your website's "Launch" page and post it in your social media and chat groups a few times before the big day.

Step 4: Build Hype Through Social Channels

Using Social Media:

- **Twitter and Telegram:** Post countdowns, reminders, and teaser images. Show off your logo, memes, and any promotional materials you've designed.

- **Discord or Community Chats:** Host live chats or Q&A sessions to get people excited and answer their last-minute questions.

Influencers and Partnerships:

If possible, consider reaching out to small influencers or popular meme accounts that align with your theme. A friendly mention or retweet can draw more eyes to your launch event.

Step 5: Ensure Technical Preparedness

Check Your Smart Contract and Liquidity:

- **Smart Contract Audit (If Possible):** A quick code review, even if informal, can reassure people that the contract is safe.

- **Liquidity Pool Setup:** If you're adding liquidity (tokens and some of the network's native currency) to a decentralized exchange, have this ready just before launch. This ensures people can actually trade right when you go live.

Prepare for High Traffic:

If your website is hosting the launch information, make sure it can handle a sudden surge in visitors. Check that all links and instructions are correct and easy to follow.

Step 6: Launch, Monitor, and Celebrate

Launching on the Big Day:

- **Announce the Launch:** Post a "We Are Live!" update across all your social channels at the exact launch time.

- **Monitor Transactions:** Watch the blockchain explorer (like Etherscan for Ethereum) to see the first transactions roll in. This helps confirm that everything's working smoothly.

Engage With Your Community Post-Launch:

- **Answer Questions:** Some people might get stuck or need help. Be patient and guide them.

- **Show Gratitude:** Thank everyone for their support and encourage them to share their experience with friends.

Step 7: Reflect and Improve

Gather Feedback:

Ask your community what went well and what could be improved. Did they find the instructions clear? Was the process fair?

Adjust for the Future:

If you plan to launch more features or future projects, use this feedback to make your next launch even smoother and more welcoming to newcomers.

In conclusion, building and engaging a strong community is paramount for the success of meme coins. A vibrant and active community not only drives value and credibility but also fosters a sense of belonging and enthusiasm among investors and supporters. By creating official communication channels such as Discord, Telegram, Reddit, and integrated tweet trackers, you can provide real-time updates and facilitate ongoing engagement. Developing a content strategy that includes regular updates, interactive content, and educational posts keeps the community informed and entertained. Additionally, fostering community participation through contests, airdrops, gamified incentives, and verified giveaways helps to strengthen loyalty and attract new members. Managing community feedback and actively listening to their suggestions and concerns allows for continuous improvement and demonstrates a commitment to a thriving community. By prioritizing community-building efforts, you can cultivate an enthusiastic and supportive community that propels your meme coin towards greater success.

Chapter 4
Building and Engaging Your Community

Building a strong and engaged community is paramount for the success of any meme coin. In this chapter, we will explore the importance of community in meme coins and how it drives value and credibility. We will delve into the strategies for creating official communication channels, developing a content strategy, fostering community participation, and managing community feedback. By prioritizing community-building efforts, you can cultivate an enthusiastic and supportive community that propels your meme coin towards greater success. So, let's dive in and discover the key steps to building and engaging your community in the world of meme coins.

Importance of Community in Meme Coins: How Community Drives Value and Credibility

In the world of meme coins, the community plays a pivotal role in driving the value and credibility of the coin. The community acts as the backbone, driving enthusiasm, and creating a sense of belonging among investors. Here are a few key ways in which the community influences the success of meme coins:

1. Market Perception and Trust: A vibrant and engaged community instills confidence and trust in potential investors. When a meme coin has an active and supportive community, it signals that there is genuine interest and belief in the project, attracting more investors and contributing to the coin's overall value.

2. Liquidity and Trading Volume: A strong community can lead to increased liquidity and trading volume. With a dedicated community actively buying, selling, and trading the meme coin, it creates a more vibrant marketplace and enhances liquidity, making it easier for investors to enter or exit their positions.

3. Network Effects and Virality: Meme coins thrive on virality, and a passionate community is instrumental in driving this phenomenon. When community members share and promote the coin across social media platforms, it can generate widespread attention, attracting new investors and driving up the coin's value.

4. Long-Term Support and Development: A committed community provides ongoing support and contributes to the development of the meme coin. Community members often offer valuable insights, help identify bugs or issues, and suggest new features, creating an ecosystem of continuous improvement and innovation.

5. Community-Driven Initiatives: Community-driven initiatives such as collaborations, partnerships, and charity efforts can further enhance the value and credibility of a meme coin. These initiatives not only foster goodwill but also attract attention from outside investors and increase the coin's visibility in the broader market.

In summary, the community is a crucial factor in the success of meme coins. It drives value and credibility by fostering trust, enhancing liquidity, amplifying virality, providing ongoing support, and spearheading community-driven initiatives. As meme coins continue to capture attention in the cryptocurrency space, nurturing and engaging the community should be a top priority for their long-term success.

Creating Official Communication Channels

Establishing official communication channels is crucial for meme coins to foster a thriving community and ensure effective and transparent communication. These channels serve as platforms for disseminating updates, interacting with community members, addressing queries, and building trust. Here are some key communication channels that meme coin projects should consider:

Discord: Discord is a popular messaging and community platform that allows for real-time communication, voice chats, and the creation of various channels dedicated to different topics or purposes. It provides a space for community members to connect, ask questions, share ideas, and engage in discussions.

Telegram: Similar to Discord, Telegram is a widely used messaging platform that enables the creation of groups and channels. It provides a convenient way for meme coin projects to broadcast announcements, share updates, and have direct interactions with the community.

Reddit: Reddit is a social news aggregation and discussion platform with various communities known as subreddits. Creating an official subreddit for the meme coin project allows for community engagement, sharing updates, and fostering discussions among community members.

Integrated Tweet Trackers: Integrated tweet trackers help meme coin projects monitor and display relevant tweets about the project in real-time. This allows community members to stay updated on the latest news and discussions surrounding the coin.

By utilizing these official communication channels, meme coin projects can establish a strong presence, facilitate transparent communication, and build a sense of community among their supporters.

Here are some valuable step by step instructions on how to create your official communication channels:

Step 1: Pick the Right Platforms

Begin by choosing which platforms best suit your community. For real-time chats and organized discussions, start a **Discord server**. For quick updates that people can check on their phones, create a **Telegram group**. To host longer posts and encourage community-driven content, set up a **Reddit subreddit**. By using all three, you'll give community members multiple ways to stay informed and engaged. Consider integrating a **tweet tracker** into your Discord or Telegram so that each time you post a new tweet, everyone gets notified automatically.

Step 2: Keep Your Branding Consistent

Use your meme coin's name, logo, and colors across every channel. Make sure your Discord server's icon matches your Twitter profile picture and that your subreddit banner shows off your brand's color scheme. This consistency helps people instantly recognize that they're in the right place and dealing with the official channels.

Step 3: Post Essential Information in Easy-to-Find Spots

At the top of your Discord, pin a message with vital information—your official website link, token contract address, and social media profiles. Do the same in your Telegram group's description and as a pinned post on your subreddit. Having all the basic info front and center reduces confusion for newcomers and gives them confidence that they're in an official space.

Step 4: Set Clear Rules and Guidelines

Before inviting lots of people, write simple rules that explain what's allowed in your channels. For example, no spam, no hateful comments, and no scams. Post these rules in a pinned message on Discord, as a "Welcome" topic on Reddit, and in your Telegram group's info. Clear guidelines keep your community friendly, respectful, and focused on your meme coin's goals.

Step 5: Add Moderators or Trusted Helpers

Ask a few reliable community members to help moderate. They can greet newcomers, answer basic questions, remove spam, and ensure everyone follows the rules. Having a small team of helpers makes your channels feel more welcoming and professional.

Step 6: Regularly Update and Engage

Don't let your channels go silent. Post regular updates about your meme coin's progress, upcoming events, or new features. On Discord and Reddit, consider hosting Q&A sessions or "Ask Me Anything" chats. On Telegram, share quick news briefs. Use the tweet tracker you integrated so your community gets notified whenever you post on Twitter, keeping them in the loop no matter where they spend their time.

Step 7: Encourage Community Participation

Invite members to create and share their own memes, ask questions, or start discussions. Consider running small contests for the best fan art or most helpful posts. When the community feels like they're part of the project's story, they're more likely to stick around and help spread the word.

Step 8: Listen and Adjust

Pay attention to what people say. If you notice the same question keeps popping up, update your pinned information to make it clearer. If your community prefers one platform over another, invest more time there. Don't be afraid to ask your members what else they'd like to see. Over time, you can fine-tune your communication strategy based on their feedback.

By following these steps, you'll create easy-to-navigate, informative, and welcoming communication channels for your meme coin. This helps build trust, encourages sharing, and keeps everyone connected—key ingredients to making your project a lasting success.

Why Multiple Platforms Matter

When it comes to promoting your meme coin and keeping your supporters in the loop, relying on just one platform won't cut it. Your community members will have their own preferences—some enjoy real-time chats, others prefer a more traditional forum style, and some simply rely on social media feeds. By spreading your presence across platforms like Discord, Telegram, and Reddit, and by integrating tweet trackers, you ensure that everyone can stay connected in the way they prefer. This not only makes your project more accessible but also helps it reach a wider audience.

Setting Up a Discord Server

What Is Discord and Why Use It?

Discord is a chat platform where you can create your own server, host multiple text and voice channels, and manage discussions with ease. It feels like a virtual hangout where your community can gather and talk in real time. For meme coins, a well-structured Discord server can foster community spirit, help newcomers learn the ropes, and encourage long-time supporters to stay active and engaged.

How to Get Started:

1. **Create a Server:** Sign up for Discord, click "Add a Server," and choose a name and icon that reflect your meme coin's branding.

2. **Organize Channels:** Set up separate text channels for announcements, general chat, memes, support questions, and development updates. You can also host voice channels for live hangouts, Q&A sessions, or listening parties to celebrate milestones.

3. **Pin Essential Info:** In your #announcements channel, pin a message that includes a link to your website, contract address, and social media handles. Doing this upfront makes your server more user-friendly.

Moderation and Bots:

- **Roles and Permissions:** Assign roles like "Moderator" or "Community Manager" to trusted individuals who can keep the server clean, remove spam, and answer common questions.

- **Useful Bots:** Consider adding a bot that can welcome new members, post automatic reminders about rules, or even help with automated polls and community votes.

Utilizing Telegram for Quick Updates

What Is Telegram and Why Use It?

Telegram is a popular messaging app known for its simplicity, speed, and large user base. Many crypto enthusiasts already use Telegram to follow projects. Setting up a Telegram channel or group for your meme coin means you can broadcast updates instantly, and your members can check in easily on their phones.

How to Get Started:

1. **Create a Group or Channel:** Decide if you want a channel (one-way communication where only you post updates) or a group (where everyone can chat). A channel is great for official announcements, while a group encourages conversation.

2. **Link to Discord and Other Platforms:** In the description of your Telegram group, provide links to your Discord, Reddit, and Twitter. This creates a cycle of discovery and helps new members find all your communication hubs.

3. **Short, Snappy Updates:** Telegram is often checked "on the go," so keep messages short and to the point. Use it to announce new developments, remind people of upcoming events, or highlight big community achievements.

Simple Moderation:

Unlike Discord's complexity, Telegram's moderation tools are simpler. You can assign admins, turn on slow mode to limit spam, and quickly remove unwanted messages. Consider adding a Telegram bot for auto-moderation or to answer common FAQs, ensuring new members feel supported from the start.

Building a Reddit Community

What Is Reddit and Why Use It?

Reddit is a forum-like platform where users submit posts, comment, and upvote or downvote content. Creating a subreddit for your meme coin allows for deeper discussions than quick chats on Discord or Telegram. It's a great space to host longer-form content, community guides, detailed updates, and in-depth Q&A threads.

How to Get Started:

1. **Create a Subreddit:** You'll need a Reddit account. After logging in, you can create your own subreddit. Choose a name that matches your meme coin brand, and customize the look with banners and your logo.

2. **Pinned Posts and Sidebars:** At the top of your subreddit, pin a "Welcome" post that introduces your coin, explains your mission, and provides essential links. Use the subreddit's sidebar to display rules, helpful resources, and social links.

3. **Encourage User-Generated Content:** Reddit thrives on community involvement. Ask your members to post their own memes, questions, and ideas. Consider hosting weekly discussion threads or spotlighting community contributions in a recurring feature post.

Moderation and Engagement:

Reddit moderation tools let you remove spam, set filters for suspicious posts, and create specific rules for acceptable content. Engaging regularly—answering questions, commenting on posts, and occasionally hosting AMA (Ask Me Anything) sessions—helps keep the community lively and shows you're listening.

Integrating Tweet Trackers

What Are Tweet Trackers and Why Use Them?

A tweet tracker is a tool (often a bot) that automatically posts updates to your chosen platforms whenever you tweet. It's an easy way to ensure that vital announcements on Twitter don't go unnoticed by community members who aren't always checking social media.

How to Get Started:

1. **Choose a Bot or Integration Tool:** Look for Discord or Telegram bots that can track specific Twitter accounts. They usually require a few setup steps: granting access, specifying which account to follow, and choosing a channel to post updates.

2. **Automate Alerts:** Once set up, the bot will automatically share your tweets in a designated Discord channel or Telegram group. This means every announcement, price update, or partnership reveal you make on Twitter will instantly reach your Discord and Telegram communities.

3. **Combine With Pinned Info:** Mention your tweet channel or feed in your pinned posts, so newcomers know that's where to find the latest news. This encourages them to pay attention to key updates.

Why This Matters:

Not everyone uses Twitter, but many projects share their biggest news there first. By integrating a tweet tracker, you ensure that your Discord and Telegram followers never miss a major announcement. It makes your communication more seamless and less dependent on a single platform.

Bringing It All Together

By leveraging Discord, Telegram, Reddit, and integrated tweet trackers, you create a comprehensive communication ecosystem. Here's how it might look in practice:

- **Discord** is your hub for real-time chat, community hangouts, and voice events.

- **Telegram** delivers quick updates and lightweight communication on mobile devices.

- **Reddit** hosts longer, more detailed discussions, community polls, and knowledge-building posts.

- **Tweet Trackers** ensure that important announcements on Twitter are instantly shared with everyone, so no crucial info slips through the cracks.

This multi-channel approach lets your community choose their preferred way of staying informed. It also reduces friction—those who love chatting can stick to Discord, while those who want more structured content can rely on Reddit. Meanwhile, telegram fans can get pinged on their phones, and tweet trackers ensure no one misses a beat.

Tips for Long-Term Success

1. **Stay Consistent:** Post regularly and respond to questions in a timely manner. Inactive or neglected channels discourage members from sticking around.

2. **Be Transparent:** The more honest and open you are about project updates, the more trust you build. Address challenges or delays openly, and thank your community for their support.

3. **Encourage Participation:** Contests, community questions, polls, and themed events can keep your members excited and eager to contribute content of their own.

4. **Adapt and Evolve:** Pay attention to what works best. If Discord is buzzing while Reddit is quiet, consider investing more effort in Discord and using Reddit for special posts or announcements. Over

time, refine your strategy to meet the needs of your growing community.

In essence, by maintaining a presence on multiple platforms and using tools like tweet trackers, you'll create an inclusive, well-informed, and engaged community around your meme coin. This approach forms the foundation of a thriving project, ensuring that your supporters always know where to find updates, ask questions, and celebrate successes together.

Important – For The Meme-Coin Investor

Leveraging Social Media Platforms: Twitter (X), Instagram, TikTok—Enhanced with Tweet Tracker Tools for Real-Time Insights

If you're looking to buy into meme coins and want to separate reliable projects from those that are less trustworthy, social media can be a powerful research tool. By following official announcements, engaging with community posts, and paying close attention to the creators' transparency, you can gain a better understanding of which meme coins deserve a closer look. With platforms like Twitter (recently rebranded as X), Instagram, and TikTok—and the help of tweet tracker tools—you can keep up with the latest developments and gauge the legitimacy of a project before making a purchase.

Why Social Media Matters for Buyers:
Meme coin communities often begin and thrive on social networks. This is where developers and influencers share milestones, address concerns, and respond to feedback. By following these channels, you can observe how consistently the team communicates, whether they respond to tough questions, and how supportive their fan base is. Over time, you'll gain

insights into a project's credibility, growth potential, and the level of trust it has earned within the community.

Twitter (X) for Real-Time Announcements:

Most meme coin teams rely heavily on Twitter (X) for quick updates and breaking news. By following their official accounts, you can stay informed about new partnerships, upcoming token burns, exchange listings, and other moves that might affect the coin's value. To save time and ensure you never miss an important post, consider integrating a tweet tracker—a tool that sends you instant notifications whenever the project's official account tweets. This is especially valuable since key announcements often appear on Twitter first, allowing you to act quickly when new information emerges.

Instagram for Visual Branding and Trust Signals:

While Twitter (X) is great for rapid-fire updates, Instagram offers a more visual perspective. Developers may share behind-the-scenes glimpses of their team, show off merchandise, or highlight community events through photos and stories. For a buyer, seeing the faces behind a project or proof of real-world meetups can help confirm that the team and community are genuine, not just anonymous avatars. Pay attention to how active the account is, whether they engage with their audience in the comments, and if the content looks professionally managed. A consistent, authentic Instagram presence is often a good sign that a project is invested in its long-term reputation.

TikTok for Community Vibes and Creator Accountability:

TikTok's short videos can capture the tone of a project's community in seconds. Influencers and team members might produce quick updates, educational content, or humorous skits related to the meme coin. By scrolling through their feed, you can see if there's real enthusiasm and creativity coming from both creators and followers. If you notice that the same influencer repeatedly supports reputable projects, it can signal that they do their due diligence. On the flip side, if you see a sudden flood of videos about a coin from unfamiliar accounts making unrealistic claims, you might want to tread carefully.

Evaluating Legitimacy and Transparency:

Social media is a double-edged sword—it's easy for anyone to post big promises or polished marketing, but it's also easier for the community to spot inconsistencies. Keep an eye out for:

- **Consistent Messaging:** Are the project's statements across Twitter, Instagram, and TikTok consistent, or do they contradict each other?

- **Team Visibility:** Does the team reveal their real names, backgrounds, or previous work experience? Genuine projects often have team members who proudly showcase their involvement.

- **Community Interaction:** Do creators and project leads respond to questions, or do they dodge them? Regular engagement and honest dialogue are strong indicators that they're invested in the project's future.

- **Use Your Tweet Tracker Wisely:** Set alerts for trusted influencers, auditors, and analysts who review meme coins. When they post about a project, check if they highlight transparency and clear communication as strengths.

Adjusting Your Strategy Over Time

As you gain experience navigating these platforms, you'll develop a better sense of which social signals truly matter. If your tweet tracker shows a project posting regular, substantive updates and engaging positively with critical questions, it likely warrants further research. If the social presence feels forced, overly pro-

motional, or evasive, you might decide to look elsewhere.

In the end, leveraging social media platforms—combined with tweet tracker tools—can give you a front-row seat to the story behind each meme coin. By paying close attention to the authenticity, consistency, and depth of information shared across Twitter (X), Instagram, and TikTok, you'll become more confident in identifying legitimate projects and steering clear of those that don't measure up.

Chapter 5
Marketing and Promoting Your Meme Coin

Creating a successful meme coin goes beyond the technical aspects of blockchain and token creation. To thrive in the highly competitive cryptocurrency market, especially within the meme coin niche, a robust and comprehensive marketing plan is essential. This guide will walk you through the key components of developing such a plan, addressing both creators and investors. We'll cover setting goals, measuring return on investment (ROI), integrating blockchain verification as a trust signal, utilizing social media, forming influencer partnerships, content marketing, paid advertising, email marketing, public relations, virtual events, community incentives, and analyzing your marketing efforts. By the end of this guide, you'll have a clear roadmap to effectively market your meme coin and engage your community.

Setting Goals, Measuring ROI, and Integrating Blockchain Verification as a Trust Signal

For Creators

Setting Clear Goals: As a meme coin creator, your first step is to define what success looks like for your project. Are you aiming for a certain number of token holders, a specific market cap, or widespread recognition within the crypto community? Clear, measurable goals help guide your marketing efforts and keep your team focused.

Measuring ROI: Return on Investment (ROI) is crucial to understanding the effectiveness of your marketing campaigns. Track metrics such as engagement rates, conversion rates, and overall growth in token holders. Tools like Google Analytics, social media insights, and blockchain explorers can provide valuable data to assess the impact of your marketing activities.

Integrating Blockchain Verification: Blockchain verification serves as a trust signal to potential investors. By making your smart contracts publicly verifiable, you enhance transparency and build trust within your community. Ensure that your token's contract is audited and the audit results are easily accessible. Highlight these verifications in your marketing materials to reassure investors of your project's legitimacy.

For Investors

Understanding Creator Goals: As an investor, it's important to understand the goals set by the meme coin creators. Are they realistic and achievable? Goals provide insight into the project's direction and potential for growth.

Evaluating ROI Metrics: Look for projects that transparently share their ROI metrics. High engagement rates, consistent growth in token holders, and positive community feedback are indicators of a healthy investment. Use blockchain explorers to verify these metrics independently.

Trust Through Blockchain Verification: Investors should prioritize meme coins with verified smart contracts and audited codes. This reduces the risk of scams and ensures that the token operates as intended. Always check for publicly available audit reports before investing.

Utilizing Social Media for Promotion

Strategies for X (Twitter), Discord, Reddit, Telegram

Twitter (X): Twitter remains a pivotal platform for cryptocurrency promotion due to its real-time nature and broad reach. Creators should use Twitter to announce updates, share news, and engage with the community. Regular tweets, retweets, and interactions with followers can help build a loyal following. Utilize hashtags relevant to crypto and meme coins to increase visibility.

Discord: Discord serves as a hub for community building and real-time interaction. Creators can set up dedicated servers with channels for announcements, general discussion, support, and memes. Hosting regular events like AMAs (Ask Me Anything) and live discussions fosters a sense of community and keeps members engaged.

Reddit: Reddit is ideal for in-depth discussions and community-driven content. Creating a subreddit for your meme coin allows users to post detailed questions, share insights, and engage in long-form conversations. Regularly participating in subreddit threads and hosting community polls can drive engagement and gather valuable feedback.

Telegram: Telegram offers a fast and direct way to communicate with your community. Setting up a Telegram group or channel allows creators to send instant updates, share important links, and facilitate quick discussions. Using Telegram bots for automated responses and updates can enhance user experience and manage large communities efficiently.

For Investors

Engaging with Communities: As an investor, actively participating in these social media platforms can provide deeper insights into the meme coin's community health and creator transparency. Engaging in discussions, asking questions, and observing community interactions can help gauge the project's legitimacy and potential for growth.

Monitoring Social Signals: Pay attention to the level of activity and positivity within these platforms. High engagement and supportive interactions are positive signs, while frequent negativity or lack of communication might be red flags.

Employing Tweet Trackers and Analytics to Catch Trends Early

Tweet Trackers: Tweet trackers are tools that monitor specific Twitter accounts for new tweets and notify you in real-time. For meme coin creators, integrating tweet trackers into Discord or Telegram ensures that community members receive immediate updates without needing to constantly check Twitter. This can be achieved using bots like TweetShift or custom webhook integrations.

Analytics Tools: Utilize analytics platforms such as Google Analytics, Twitter Analytics, and Discord Insights to track the performance of your marketing campaigns. These tools provide data on user engagement, traffic sources, and conversion rates, enabling you to refine your strategies based on what's working and what isn't.

For Investors

Early Trend Detection: Investors can use tweet trackers to stay informed about critical updates and announcements from meme coin creators. Being aware of new partnerships, token burns, or exchange listings as soon as they happen can provide a strategic advantage in making timely investment decisions.

Data-Driven Decisions: Analyzing social media trends and engagement metrics helps investors identify which meme coins have strong community support and active development. Projects with consistent positive trends are more likely to succeed, making them safer investment choices.

Influencer Partnerships and Collaborations

Identifying Authentic Influencers via Wallet Verification and Past Performance

For Creators: Partnering with influencers can amplify your meme coin's reach and credibility. However, it's essential to choose authentic influencers who align with your project's values and have a genuine following. Look for influencers who have a history of supporting legitimate projects and whose audience engages meaningfully with their content.

Wallet Verification: To ensure influencers are authentic, verify their wallet addresses to confirm they hold and have transacted with your meme coin. This demonstrates their genuine interest and support for your project, rather than a paid endorsement without real investment.

Past Performance: Review the influencer's past collaborations and their outcomes. Successful partnerships with other crypto projects indicate reliability and effectiveness. Analyze their engagement rates, audience demographics, and the quality of their content to ensure they can deliver value to your marketing efforts.

For Investors

Evaluating Influencer Credibility: When considering investing in a meme coin, assess the credibility of the influencers promoting it. Authentic influencers who transparently support the project and have a history of promoting legitimate coins add credibility and reduce the risk of falling for pump-and-dump schemes.

Wallet Verification and Transparency: Check if the influencers genuinely hold the meme coin they're promoting. This can be done by examining their wallet transactions on blockchain explorers. Authentic endorsements from verified holders indicate genuine support and trust in the project.

Content Marketing and SEO

Creating Valuable Content and Using Data-Backed Insights from Blockchain Metrics

For Creators: Content marketing involves creating and sharing valuable content to attract and engage your target audience. For meme coins, this can include blog posts, videos, infographics, and social media content that explain your project's vision, tokenomics, and unique selling points.

SEO (Search Engine Optimization): Optimize your content for search engines to increase visibility. Use relevant keywords related to meme coins and your specific project. Regularly update your website and blog with fresh content to improve your search rankings and drive organic traffic.

Data-Backed Insights: Leverage blockchain metrics to create informative content. Share data on token distribution, transaction volumes, and holder statistics to provide transparency and build trust. Use these insights to create detailed reports, whitepapers, and visual data presentations that highlight your project's strengths and growth potential.

For Investors

Informative Content Consumption: As an investor, consuming high-quality content helps you make informed decisions. Look for projects that provide detailed explanations of their tokenomics, use cases, and roadmap. Well-crafted content indicates a serious and transparent team.

SEO and Discoverability: Projects that invest in SEO and content marketing are more likely to attract organic interest and grow steadily. High search rankings and comprehensive content suggest a well-managed project with a focus on long-term success.

Paid Advertising Campaigns

Using Targeted Ads While Maintaining Transparency and Ethical Promotion

For Creators: Paid advertising can significantly boost your meme coin's visibility. Platforms like Google Ads, Facebook Ads, and crypto-specific ad networks offer targeted advertising options to reach your desired audience.

Targeted Ads: Identify your target demographic and tailor your ads accordingly. Use detailed targeting options to reach crypto enthusiasts, meme culture followers, and specific geographic regions where crypto adoption is high. A/B testing different ad creatives and messages can help identify the most effective strategies.

Transparency and Ethics: Maintain transparency in your advertising campaigns. Clearly disclose partnerships, sponsorships, and the nature of your ads to build trust. Avoid misleading claims or exaggerated promises, as these can damage your project's reputation and lead to regulatory issues.

For Investors

Assessing Ad Quality and Transparency: Evaluate the quality and transparency of a meme coin's advertising efforts. Ethical promotions and clear messaging indicate a trustworthy project. Be cautious of ads that make unrealistic promises or use high-pressure sales tactics.

Targeted Advertising Insights: Understanding where a meme coin is advertising can provide insights into its target market and growth strategy. Projects that effectively use targeted ads to reach relevant audiences are more likely to attract dedicated and engaged communities.

Email Marketing and Newsletters

Regular, Trusted Updates Backed by On-Chain Data

For Creators: Email marketing remains a powerful tool for maintaining direct communication with your community. Create a mailing list by encouraging website visitors to subscribe to newsletters. Regularly send out updates, announcements, and exclusive content to keep your subscribers informed and engaged.

Trusted Updates: Ensure your newsletters provide valuable information, such as project milestones, upcoming events, and detailed analyses of on-chain data like transaction volumes and token distribution. Use these updates to reinforce transparency and build trust with your community.

On-Chain Data Integration: Incorporate on-chain data into your email content to provide factual and verifiable information. For example, include charts showing token holder distribution, recent transactions, or liquidity pool statistics. This not only adds credibility but also helps investors make informed decisions based on concrete data.

For Investors

Subscribing to Newsletters: Investors should subscribe to official newsletters to receive timely updates and in-depth information about their investments. Regular emails from a meme coin project can provide valuable insights into the project's progress and future plans.

Evaluating Information Quality: Assess the quality of the information provided in newsletters. Look for detailed explanations, transparent data presentations, and honest assessments of project developments. High-quality newsletters indicate a project's commitment to keeping its community well-informed and engaged.

Public Relations and Media Outreach

Getting Featured in Reputable Crypto News Outlets with Verified Proof of Liquidity and Trading Volume

For Creators: Public relations (PR) is essential for building your meme coin's reputation and gaining exposure in the wider crypto community. Start by crafting a compelling press release that highlights your project's unique features, milestones, and future plans. Distribute this release to reputable crypto news outlets, such as CoinDesk, CoinTelegraph, and CryptoSlate.

Verified Proof: When reaching out to media outlets, provide verified proof of liquidity and trading volume. This includes sharing blockchain data, audit reports, and verified metrics from blockchain explorers. Demonstrating transparency and providing concrete data helps establish your project's legitimacy and increases the likelihood of media coverage.

Building Relationships: Develop relationships with journalists and influencers in the crypto space. Regularly engage with them through social media, attend industry events, and offer exclusive insights or interviews. Building a network of trusted media contacts can lead to more consistent and favorable coverage.

For Investors

Seeking Reputable Media Coverage: As an investor, prioritize meme coins that receive coverage from reputable media outlets. Articles in well-known publications can provide third-party validation and reduce the risk of investing in fraudulent projects.

Verifying Proof of Liquidity: Before investing, verify the proof of liquidity and trading volume shared by the project. Use blockchain explorers to independently confirm the data presented in media coverage and ensure that the project maintains sufficient liquidity to support trading activities.

Hosting and Participating in Virtual Events

Webinars, AMAs, Leveraging Alpha Groups for Promotion

For Creators: Hosting virtual events such as webinars and AMAs (Ask Me Anything) can significantly boost your meme coin's visibility and engage your community. Webinars can be used to explain your project in detail, showcase upcoming features, and address community questions in real-time.

AMAs: AMAs on platforms like Reddit, Discord, and Telegram allow the team to interact directly with the community. These sessions build trust, provide transparency, and allow creators to address any concerns or questions investors might have. Regularly scheduled AMAs keep the community engaged and informed.

Alpha Groups: Alpha groups are exclusive communities where members receive early access to information and insights about your meme coin. By leveraging these groups, creators can reward loyal supporters and encourage word-of-mouth promotion. These groups can also serve as a source of valuable feedback and ideas from dedicated community members.

For Investors

Participating in Events: Investors should actively participate in webinars and AMAs to gain a deeper understanding of the projects they're interested in. These events offer direct access to the creators and provide an opportunity to ask questions and assess the team's transparency and responsiveness.

Assessing Event Quality: Evaluate the quality of virtual events by observing the level of detail provided, the honesty of responses, and the overall engagement from the team. High-quality events indicate a serious and dedicated project, while poorly managed events might signal underlying issues.

Community Incentives and Rewards

Airdrops, Staking Rewards, Referral Programs—with Smart Contracts Publicly Verifiable

For Creators: Incentivizing your community through airdrops, staking rewards, and referral programs can drive engagement and attract new investors. Airdrops involve distributing free tokens to your community members, often in exchange for simple tasks like following your social media accounts or joining your Discord server.

Staking Rewards: Implement staking mechanisms where holders can lock up their tokens in return for rewards. This not only incentivizes holding but also contributes to the token's stability by reducing circulating supply.

Referral Programs: Encourage your community to refer new investors by offering rewards for successful referrals. This can rapidly expand your token's reach and build a loyal supporter base.

Smart Contract Verification: Ensure that all incentive programs are governed by smart contracts that are publicly verifiable. This enhances transparency and trust, as community members can independently verify the fairness and security of the reward mechanisms.

For Investors

Participating in Incentives: Investors should take advantage of airdrops, staking rewards, and referral programs to maximize their returns. These incentives provide additional value beyond the token's price appreciation and can enhance overall investment profitability.

Verifying Reward Mechanisms: Before participating in any incentive program, verify the associated smart contracts to ensure they are secure and transparent. Use blockchain explorers to review contract code and confirm that the rules for rewards are fair and cannot be manipulated.

Measuring and Analyzing Marketing Efforts

Using Analytics Platforms and Blockchain Data to Refine Strategies

For Creators: Measuring and analyzing your marketing efforts is crucial for understanding what works and what doesn't. Utilize analytics platforms such as Google Analytics for website traffic, social media analytics for engagement metrics, and blockchain explorers for on-chain data like transaction volumes and token distribution.

Refining Strategies: Use the insights gained from these analytics to refine your marketing strategies. For instance, if certain social media campaigns generate high engagement, allocate more resources to those channels. If specific types of content drive more traffic, create similar content to maintain momentum.

Continuous Improvement: Regularly review your marketing performance and adjust your strategies based on data-driven insights. Implement A/B testing for different marketing approaches, experiment with new channels, and stay updated with the latest marketing trends in the crypto space.

For Investors

Monitoring Marketing Effectiveness: Investors should monitor the effectiveness of a meme coin's marketing efforts to gauge the project's growth potential. High engagement rates and positive marketing metrics can indicate strong community support and potential for price appreciation.

Using Blockchain Data: Analyze on-chain data to assess the project's health. Metrics such as active wallet addresses, transaction volumes, and liquidity pools provide a deeper understanding of the token's adoption and stability. Projects with consistent on-chain activity are more likely to sustain long-term growth.

Making Data-Driven Investments: By combining marketing analytics with blockchain data, investors can make informed decisions about which meme coins to invest in. Projects with robust marketing strategies and strong on-chain metrics are typically more reliable and have higher growth potential.

Developing a comprehensive marketing plan for your meme coin involves a multifaceted approach that integrates goal setting, ROI measurement, blockchain verification, social media utilization, influencer partnerships, content marketing, paid advertising, email marketing, public relations, virtual events, community incentives, and continuous analysis. For creators, this means strategically planning and executing each component to build a strong, engaged community and ensure the long-term success of the project. For investors, understanding these marketing strategies provides valuable insights into a meme coin's potential and legitimacy, enabling more informed investment decisions.

By following this guide, both creators and investors can navigate the complex landscape of meme coin marketing effectively. Creators can build and sustain a thriving community, while investors can identify and support projects with genuine potential. In the dynamic world of cryptocurrencies, a well-executed marketing plan is a key driver of success, transforming a simple meme coin into a recognized and trusted digital asset.

Chapter 6

Listing Your Meme Coin on Exchanges

Launching a meme coin involves not only creating the token but also ensuring it's accessible to potential investors through various cryptocurrency exchanges. Exchanges are platforms where users can buy, sell, and trade digital assets. Understanding the different types of exchanges and how they operate is crucial for both creators and investors to navigate the crypto landscape effectively. In the context of Pump.fun, a platform designed to streamline the creation and promotion of meme coins, this section delves into the nuances of centralized and decentralized exchanges, the role of verification tools like PumpVision, and the strategic steps required for successful exchange listings.

Centralized vs. Decentralized Exchanges

Centralized Exchanges (CEXs)

Centralized exchanges (CEXs) are traditional platforms where a central authority manages all transactions and holds users' funds. Examples include Binance, Coinbase, and Kraken. These exchanges offer high liquidity, a wide range of trading pairs, and user-friendly interfaces, making them popular among both novice and experienced traders.

Advantages of CEXs:

- **High Liquidity:** Facilitates large trades without significantly affecting the token's price.

- **User-Friendly:** Intuitive interfaces and customer support make trading accessible.

- **Advanced Features:** Offer tools like margin trading, futures, and staking.

- **Regulatory Compliance:** Often comply with regulations, enhancing security and trust.

Disadvantages of CEXs:

- **Centralization Risk:** Funds are held by the exchange, posing potential security risks if the exchange is hacked.

- **Listing Fees:** High costs associated with getting a token listed.

- **Regulatory Scrutiny:** Subject to strict regulations, which can impact operations and availability.

Decentralized Exchanges (DEXs)

Decentralized exchanges (DEXs) operate without a central authority, allowing users to trade directly from their wallets. Popular DEXs include Uniswap, PancakeSwap, and Solana-based platforms like Serum. These exchanges prioritize privacy and decentralization, aligning with the core principles of blockchain technology.

Advantages of DEXs:

- **Decentralization:** Users retain control of their funds, reducing the risk of exchange hacks.

- **Lower Barriers to Entry:** Easier and often free to list tokens, fostering innovation.

- **Privacy:** Enhanced privacy as no personal information is required.

- **24/7 Availability:** Operate continuously without downtime.

Disadvantages of DEXs:

- **Lower Liquidity:** Can result in higher price volatility and slippage.

- **User Experience:** Often less intuitive and require a higher level of technical knowledge.

- **Limited Features:** Fewer trading options and tools compared to CEXs.

- **Smart Contract Risks:** Vulnerabilities in smart contracts can lead to exploits.

Role of Verification Tools Like PumpVision for DEX Analysis

PumpVision is a specialized tool integrated with Pump.fun that provides comprehensive analysis and verification for decentralized exchanges (DEXs). It helps creators and investors assess the legitimacy, liquidity, and overall health of a DEX, ensuring informed decision-making.

Key Features of PumpVision:

- **Liquidity Analysis:** Evaluates the liquidity pools on various DEXs, ensuring there is sufficient liquidity for smooth trading.

- **Security Audits:** Checks for smart contract vulnerabilities and verifies that the DEX adheres to security best practices.

- **Performance Metrics:** Tracks trading volumes, price stability, and user activity to gauge the exchange's performance.

- **Transparency Checks:** Ensures that all transactions and liquidity provisions are transparent and verifiable on the blockchain.

Benefits for Creators:

- **Informed Listing Decisions:** Helps determine which DEXs are most suitable for listing your meme coin based on liquidity and security.

- **Risk Mitigation:** Identifies potential risks associated with specific DEXs, allowing creators to avoid platforms that may jeopardize their project.

- **Enhanced Credibility:** Listing on verified and reputable DEXs builds trust with investors and the broader community.

Benefits for Investors:

- **Due Diligence:** Provides investors with detailed insights into the exchanges they use, ensuring they trade on secure and reliable platforms.

- **Market Insights:** Offers real-time data and analytics to help investors make informed trading decisions.

- **Risk Assessment:** Helps identify and avoid exchanges with poor liquidity or security issues, safeguarding investments.

Preparing for Exchange Listings

Successfully listing your meme coin on exchanges involves careful preparation to meet technical and legal prerequisites, ensure transparent token distribution, and demonstrate the project's legitimacy. Whether targeting centralized or decentralized exchanges, following a structured approach is essential for a smooth and credible listing process.

Technical and Legal Prerequisites

Technical Requirements

Before applying to list your meme coin on any exchange, ensure that all technical aspects of your token are in order. This includes:

- **Smart Contract Audits:** Conduct thorough audits of your smart contracts to identify and fix vulnerabilities. Providing audited contracts to exchanges can enhance your project's credibility.

- **Token Standards Compliance:** Ensure your token adheres to standard protocols (e.g., ERC-20 for Ethereum-based tokens). This guarantees compatibility with various wallets and exchanges.

- **Blockchain Integration:** Verify that your token is correctly integrated with the blockchain network you intend to use. Proper integration ensures seamless transactions and interactions with the exchange's infrastructure.

Legal Requirements

Navigating the legal landscape is crucial to avoid regulatory issues that can hinder your project's growth.

- **Regulatory Compliance:** Understand the regulations governing cryptocurrency in the jurisdictions where you plan to list your token. This may involve adhering to anti-money laundering (AML) and know your customer (KYC) requirements.

- **Legal Documentation:** Prepare comprehensive legal documents, including your whitepaper, terms of service, privacy policy, and any necessary licenses or registrations.

- **Intellectual Property Protection:** Secure trademarks or patents for your meme coin's branding elements to prevent unauthorized use and protect your project's identity.

Ensuring Transparent Token Distribution

Transparency in token distribution is vital to build trust with your community and potential investors.

- **Fair Launch Practices:** Implement fair launch strategies to prevent early whales from dominating the market. This can include mechanisms like airdrops, liquidity mining, or initial DEX offerings (IDOs).

- **Verified Distribution:** Use tools like PumpVision to verify and track token distribution. Ensure that all token allocations are transparent and publicly verifiable on the blockchain.

- **Community Allocation:** Reserve a portion of tokens for community rewards, development, and marketing to demonstrate long-term commitment and sustainability.

Applying to Centralized Exchanges (CEXs)

Listing your meme coin on centralized exchanges (CEXs) can significantly enhance its visibility and accessibility. However, CEXs have stringent listing requirements and expect thorough documentation and proven liquidity. Here's how to navigate the process:

Meeting Listing Requirements and Demonstrating Verified Liquidity and Trading History

Understanding Listing Criteria: CEXs typically have specific criteria that projects must meet to be listed. These can include:

- **Project Maturity:** CEXs prefer projects that have a clear roadmap, active development, and a solid community base.

- **Liquidity:** Demonstrate sufficient liquidity to handle trading volumes without significant price volatility. This often involves showing existing liquidity pools and trading history on DEXs.

- **Compliance:** Ensure that your project complies with all relevant regulations and provides necessary legal documentation.

Demonstrating Verified Liquidity: To meet CEXs' liquidity requirements:

- **Provide Proof of Liquidity:** Use PumpVision to showcase verified liquidity pools and trading volumes. This can include screenshots from blockchain explorers or PumpVision's analytical reports.

- **Show Trading History:** If your meme coin is already traded on DEXs, provide detailed trading history and metrics to demonstrate its market presence and liquidity.

- **Liquidity Guarantees:** Consider committing a portion of your token's supply to provide initial liquidity on the CEX, ensuring a smooth trading experience for users.

Building Trading History: Establishing a trading history on DEXs before applying to CEXs can strengthen your application:

- **Consistent Trading Activity:** Ensure that your meme coin has consistent trading activity, indicating demand and interest from the community.

- **Community Engagement:** Foster an active community that regularly trades and engages with your token on DEXs, showcasing organic growth and interest.

- **Market Stability:** Maintain price stability and avoid extreme volatility through effective liquidity management and transparent communication.

Listing on Decentralized Exchanges (DEXs)

Decentralized exchanges (DEXs) offer an accessible and flexible way to list your meme coin without the stringent requirements of CEXs. Here's how to effectively list your token on popular DEXs using Pump.fun and other tools.

Setting Up Liquidity Pools on Uniswap, PancakeSwap, or Solana-based DEXs

Choosing the Right DEX: Select a DEX that aligns with your meme coin's blockchain network. Popular options include:

- **Uniswap:** Ideal for Ethereum-based tokens, offering high liquidity and a large user base.

- **PancakeSwap:** Suitable for Binance Smart Chain (BSC) tokens, known for lower transaction fees and fast processing.

- **Solana-based DEXs (e.g., Serum):** Best for Solana network tokens, providing high throughput and scalability.

Creating Liquidity Pools: To list your meme coin on a DEX, you need to create a liquidity pool:

1. **Connect Your Wallet:** Use a Web3 wallet like MetaMask, Trust Wallet, or Coinbase Wallet to connect to the DEX platform.

2. **Select Your Token Pair:** Choose a trading pair (e.g., MEME/ETH on Uniswap, MEME/BNB on PancakeSwap).

3. **Provide Liquidity:** Deposit an equal value of your meme coin and the paired asset (e.g., ETH, BNB) into the liquidity pool. This ensures that users can trade your token with sufficient liquidity.

4. **Configure Pool Parameters:** Set parameters such as fee structure and slippage tolerance based on the DEX's options and your project's needs.

5. **Launch the Pool:** Confirm the transaction in your wallet, paying the

necessary gas fees. Once the transaction

is confirmed, your meme coin is listed on the DEX and available for trading.

Using Pump.fun for DEX Integration: Pump.fun's integrated tools streamline the process of setting up and managing liquidity pools. By leveraging PumpVision, creators can analyze the optimal liquidity parameters, monitor pool performance, and ensure ongoing stability and security of their trading pairs.

Liquidity Management

Effective liquidity management is crucial for maintaining a stable trading environment and ensuring that your meme coin remains attractive to investors. Proper liquidity management involves maintaining sufficient funds in liquidity pools, monitoring for unusual trading patterns, and using tools to automate and optimize liquidity provision.

Ensuring Sufficient Liquidity

Why Liquidity Matters: Sufficient liquidity ensures that traders can buy and sell your meme coin without causing significant price fluctuations. It enhances the trading experience, reduces slippage, and attracts more investors by providing confidence in the token's market stability.

Strategies for Maintaining Liquidity:

- **Initial Liquidity Provision:** Start with a substantial initial liquidity pool to handle early trading volumes and provide a stable price foundation.

- **Ongoing Liquidity Additions:** Regularly monitor trading activity and add liquidity as needed to match increasing demand and trading volumes.

- **Liquidity Incentives:** Encourage community participation by offering incentives for liquidity providers, such as staking rewards or additional token allocations.

Using PumpVision for Liquidity Monitoring: PumpVision provides real-time analytics and monitoring tools to track the health of your liquidity pools. It alerts you to changes in liquidity levels, trading volumes, and potential liquidity drains, enabling you to take proactive measures to maintain stability.

Using Monitoring Tools to Track Suspicious Patterns

Why Monitoring is Essential: Cryptocurrency markets are susceptible to manipulative practices such as wash trading, pump-and-dump schemes, and liquidity draining. Monitoring trading patterns helps identify and mitigate these risks, protecting both your project and your investors.

Effective Monitoring Practices:

- **Transaction Analysis:** Use blockchain explorers and PumpVision to analyze transaction patterns, identifying unusual spikes or irregular trading behaviors.

- **Whale Watching:** Track large transactions and wallet movements to detect potential market manipulation by big holders.

- **Automated Alerts:** Set up automated alerts for significant changes in trading volumes, liquidity pools, or token distribution to stay informed about any suspicious activities.

Responding to Suspicious Activity:

- **Liquidity Adjustments:** If suspicious activity is detected, consider adjusting liquidity pool parameters or temporarily pausing trading to prevent further manipulation.

- **Community Transparency:** Communicate openly with your community about any detected issues and the steps being taken to address them, maintaining trust and credibility.

Maintaining Exchange Relationships

Building and maintaining strong relationships with exchanges is vital for the ongoing success of your meme coin. This involves regular communication, ensuring compliance with exchange policies, and providing transparent proof-of-reserves to reassure investors.

Regular Communication, Compliance, and Transparent Proof-of-Reserves

For Creators:

- **Open Dialogue:** Maintain consistent and open communication with exchange representatives. Regular updates about your project's progress, upcoming events, and any issues are essential for a healthy partnership.

- **Compliance Adherence:** Ensure that your project complies with the exchange's policies and regulatory requirements. This includes adhering to anti-money laundering (AML) and know your customer (KYC) protocols, as well as any specific listing guidelines.

- **Proof-of-Reserves:** Provide transparent proof-of-reserves to exchanges to demonstrate that you have sufficient funds backing your token's liquidity. This can include verified smart contract audits and regular on-chain audits using tools like PumpVision.

For Investors:

- **Trust Through Transparency:** Transparent proof-of-reserves and regular communication from creators build trust and reduce the risk of fraud or mismanagement.

- **Reliable Support:** Strong relationships between creators and exchanges often result in better support and quicker resolution of any trading issues, enhancing the overall investment experience.

Best Practices for Maintaining Relationships:

- **Timely Updates:** Keep exchanges informed about any major changes in your project, such as tokenomics adjustments, partnerships, or regulatory developments.

- **Responsive Support:** Be responsive to inquiries and requests from exchange representatives, ensuring a smooth and cooperative partnership.

- **Mutual Benefits:** Seek to create mutually beneficial relationships by exploring opportunities for joint promotions, featured listings, or exclusive trading events.

Handling Listing Fees and Costs

Listing your meme coin on exchanges involves various fees and costs that must be carefully managed to ensure financial sustainability and transparency. Proper budgeting and maintaining verifiable transaction records are essential for both creators and investors.

Budgeting Wisely with Verifiable Transaction Records

Understanding Listing Fees: Listing fees vary significantly between centralized and decentralized exchanges. CEXs typically charge substantial fees based on the token's market potential, liquidity, and the exchange's prominence. DEXs, on the other hand, often have lower or no listing fees but may require a commitment to providing liquidity.

Cost Management Strategies:

- **Initial Budget Allocation:** Allocate a specific portion of your project's budget for exchange listings, ensuring that other critical areas like development, marketing, and community incentives are also adequately funded.

- **Transparent Financial Reporting:** Maintain transparent financial records of all transactions related to listing fees and liquidity provision. Use blockchain explorers and PumpVision to provide verifiable evidence of expenditures.

- **Negotiating Fees:** When dealing with CEXs, try negotiating listing fees or exploring tiered pricing based on the token's growth and potential. Some exchanges may offer discounts or waive fees for promising projects.

For Investors:

- **Transparency in Spending:** Investors appreciate projects that demonstrate responsible financial management. Transparent reporting of listing fees and related costs reassures investors that funds are being used appropriately to drive project growth.

- **Assessing Financial Health:** Reviewing the project's budgeting for exchange listings and other expenses can provide insights into the team's financial discipline and long-term sustainability.

Promoting Exchange Listings

Successfully listing your meme coin on exchanges is only half the battle. Promoting these listings across all your communication channels, backed by on-chain data, is crucial for maximizing visibility and attracting investors.

Announcing on All Channels, Backed by On-Chain Data for Credibility

For Creators:

- **Comprehensive Announcements:** Announce your exchange listings across all your communication platforms, including Discord, Telegram, Reddit, Twitter (X), Instagram, and TikTok. Use consistent messaging to ensure that your community receives the news simultaneously.

- **On-Chain Data Integration:** Incorporate on-chain data into your announcements to provide proof of liquidity and trading history. Share blockchain explorer links or PumpVision analytics to substantiate your claims and enhance credibility.

- **Visual Content:** Create engaging visual content such as infographics, videos, and memes to accompany your announcements. Visual aids make the information more accessible and shareable, increasing the likelihood of reaching a broader audience.

For Investors:

- **Stay Informed:** Investors should follow all official channels to receive timely updates about exchange listings. This ensures they can take advantage of new trading opportunities as soon as they become available.

- **Verify Announcements:** Use on-chain data and verification tools like PumpVision to confirm the legitimacy of exchange listings. This helps avoid falling for fake announcements or scam projects.

Best Practices for Promotion:

- **Countdowns and Teasers:** Build anticipation by posting countdowns and teasers leading up to the listing date. This creates excitement and encourages community members to participate actively.

- **Live Announcements:** Host live announcement events on platforms like Discord and Telegram to engage with your community in real-time, answer questions, and celebrate the milestone together.

- **Consistent Follow-Up:** After the initial announcement, provide regular updates on the listing process, any changes in the schedule, and immediate trading results to keep the community informed and engaged.

Monitoring Exchange Performance

After your meme coin is listed on exchanges, it's essential to continuously monitor its performance to ensure ongoing success and address any emerging issues promptly. Monitoring involves tracking trading volumes, user feedback, and unusual wallet activity to maintain a healthy and stable trading environment.

Tracking Trading Volumes, User Feedback, and Unusual Wallet Activity

For Creators:

- **Trading Volume Analysis:** Use PumpVision to monitor trading volumes across different exchanges. High and stable trading volumes indicate strong market interest, while sudden spikes or drops may signal market manipulation or loss of interest.

- **User Feedback Collection:** Actively gather feedback from your community regarding the trading experience. Use surveys, polls, and direct interactions on Discord and Telegram to understand user satisfaction and identify areas for improvement.

- **Detecting Unusual Activity:** Implement monitoring tools to detect

unusual wallet activity, such as large token movements or multiple transactions from a single wallet. This helps identify potential
pump-and-dump schemes or other malicious activities that could
harm your project's reputation.

For Investors:

- **Volume Trends:** Investors should keep an eye on trading volume
  trends as they can indicate the health and popularity of a meme coin.
  Consistently rising volumes suggest growing interest, while declining
  volumes might be a red flag.

- **Community Sentiment:** Pay attention to user feedback and sentiment on social media platforms. Positive engagement and active
  discussions often correlate with a healthy project, while negative
  feedback or frequent complaints could indicate underlying issues.

- **Activity Monitoring:** Use blockchain explorers and PumpVision to
  track wallet activity and ensure there are no suspicious transactions
  that could impact the token's stability or security.

Best Practices for Monitoring:

- **Regular Reports:** Generate regular performance reports using analytics tools to track key metrics and identify trends over time.

- **Responsive Actions:** Be prepared to take immediate action if you
  detect any issues, such as increasing liquidity, enhancing security
  measures, or addressing community concerns promptly.

- **Transparent Communication:** Keep your community informed
  about the token's performance and any steps you're taking to maintain its stability and growth. Transparency builds trust and fosters a
  supportive community.

Expanding to Multiple Exchanges

Diversifying your meme coin's presence across multiple exchanges is a strategic move that broadens market access, enhances liquidity, and mitigates risks associated with being reliant on a single platform. Here's how to effectively expand your listings using Pump.fun.

Diversifying Listings for Broader Market Access and Risk Mitigation

For Creators:

- **Strategic Selection:** Choose a mix of centralized and decentralized exchanges to maximize your meme coin's exposure. Consider factors such as the exchange's user base, liquidity, security features, and compatibility with your token's blockchain.

- **Phased Listings:** Roll out your listings in phases, starting with high-impact exchanges and gradually expanding to additional platforms. This approach allows you to manage resources effectively and monitor performance before scaling up.

- **Global Reach:** Aim for listings on exchanges that cater to different geographic regions to tap into diverse markets. This increases the potential for broader adoption and reduces the risk of regional regulatory changes affecting your project.

For Investors:

- **Access to Markets:** Multiple exchange listings provide investors with more trading options and better access to different markets, enhancing the token's liquidity and price stability.

- **Risk Diversification:** Diversifying listings reduces the risk of a single exchange issue affecting the entire token's market. If one exchange faces downtime or security issues, investors can still trade on other platforms without significant disruptions.

Best Practices for Expanding Listings:

- **Market Research:** Conduct thorough research to identify the best exchanges for your meme coin based on factors like trading volume, user demographics, and platform reputation.

- **Tailored Approaches:** Customize your listing strategies for each exchange, considering their unique requirements and preferences. This increases the likelihood of successful and smooth listings.

- **Continuous Evaluation:** Regularly assess the performance of each exchange listing to ensure it aligns with your project's goals. Adjust your strategies based on performance data and market trends to optimize your listings continually.

Understanding and effectively managing exchange listings is a critical component of launching and sustaining a successful meme coin. By comprehensively navigating the differences between centralized and decentralized exchanges, leveraging tools like PumpVision for DEX analysis, and meticulously preparing for listings, creators can ensure their tokens gain the necessary visibility and liquidity. Furthermore, maintaining robust exchange relationships, managing liquidity responsibly, handling listing fees transparently, and promoting listings strategically are essential steps that contribute to a meme coin's long-term success.

For investors, a deep understanding of exchange dynamics, coupled with vigilant monitoring of trading activities and community sentiment, empowers them to make informed investment decisions and identify legitimate projects amidst the crowded crypto market. By following the structured approaches outlined in this guide, both creators and investors can navigate the complexities of exchange listings, fostering a thriving and trustworthy ecosystem for meme coins.

In the dynamic and ever-evolving world of cryptocurrencies, a well-executed exchange strategy not only enhances a meme coin's market presence but also builds the foundation for sustainable growth and community trust.

Leveraging platforms like Pump.fun and tools like PumpVision ensures that both creators and investors are equipped with the insights and resources needed to excel in this competitive landscape.

Chapter 7
Scanning and Evaluating Other Meme Coins

Investing in meme coins can be both exciting and risky due to their volatile nature and the prevalence of scams in the cryptocurrency space. To make informed investment decisions, it's essential to understand and identify the key indicators that signal a meme coin's potential for success. This comprehensive guide will walk you through these indicators, explaining how to assess community size, liquidity, development activity, smart contract security, tokenomics, team credibility, social media presence, community sentiment, transparency, and more. Utilizing tools like Pump.fun, PumpVision, and other analytical platforms will help both creators and investors navigate the complex landscape of meme coins effectively.

Community Size, Liquidity, Development Activity—Verified Through Blockchain Explorers

Community Size

For Creators: Building a large and active community is crucial for the success of a meme coin. A vibrant community not only drives demand but also fosters a sense of ownership and loyalty among its members. To grow your community:

- **Engage Regularly:** Use platforms like Discord, Telegram, and Reddit to interact with your members. Host AMAs, contests, and giveaways to keep the community engaged.

- **Provide Value:** Share regular updates, educational content, and exclusive insights to keep your community informed and invested in your project's progress.

For Investors: When evaluating a meme coin, the size and activity level of its community can provide valuable insights into its potential success.

- **Active Participation:** Look for communities with active discussions, frequent posts, and engaged members. A large number of followers on social media platforms like Twitter (X), Instagram, and TikTok can also indicate strong community support.

- **Growth Trends:** Use blockchain explorers and analytical tools like PumpVision to track the growth of the community over time. Consistent growth is a positive sign of increasing interest and trust in the project.

Liquidity

For Creators: Ensuring sufficient liquidity is essential for the smooth trading of your meme coin. High liquidity reduces price volatility and makes it easier for users to buy and sell tokens without significant price fluctuations.

- **Liquidity Pools:** Set up and maintain liquidity pools on popular decentralized exchanges (DEXs) like Uniswap, PancakeSwap, or Solana-based DEXs. Use Pump.fun's integrated tools to manage and monitor these pools effectively.

- **Incentivize Liquidity Providers:** Offer rewards such as staking bonuses or additional tokens to encourage users to add liquidity to your pools.

For Investors: Liquidity is a critical factor to consider when investing in meme coins. High liquidity ensures that you can easily enter and exit positions without facing large spreads or slippage.

- **Monitor Liquidity Levels:** Use blockchain explorers and tools like PumpVision to check the current liquidity of a meme coin. Higher liquidity typically indicates a healthier market and less susceptibility to price manipulation.

- **Check Trading Volume:** Consistent and high trading volumes are indicators of a liquid market. Low trading volumes can lead to higher volatility and difficulty in executing trades.

Development Activity

For Creators: Active and ongoing development is a strong indicator of a meme coin's commitment to growth and improvement. Regular updates, new features, and active bug fixing demonstrate the project's dedication.

- **Transparent Roadmap:** Share a clear and detailed roadmap outlining past achievements and future plans. Update it regularly to reflect progress and upcoming milestones.

- **Open Source Development:** Make your project's code available on platforms like GitHub. Encourage community contributions and maintain transparency in development activities.

For Investors: A high level of development activity can signal that the project is actively improving and expanding its features, which is crucial for long-term success.

- **GitHub Activity:** Check the project's GitHub repository for regular commits, updates, and contributions from developers. Active repositories are a positive sign of ongoing development.

- **Community Feedback:** Engage with the community on platforms like Discord and Reddit to gauge their satisfaction with the project's development progress. Positive feedback and suggestions indicate a healthy development process.

Analyzing Smart Contracts for Security

Checking Code Integrity and Audits, Using Specialized Tools Like BullX and PumpVision

For Creators: Ensuring the security of your smart contracts is paramount to building trust and protecting your community's investments.

- **Code Audits:** Have your smart contracts audited by reputable security firms. An audit report can identify vulnerabilities and provide recommendations for improvements.

- **Use Security Tools:** Utilize specialized tools like BullX and PumpVision to analyze and monitor your smart contracts. These tools can detect potential security issues and ensure ongoing contract integrity.

For Investors: Investors should thoroughly analyze a meme coin's smart contracts to assess their security and reliability.

- **Review Audit Reports:** Examine the results of third-party audits to ensure the smart contracts are secure and free from vulnerabilities. Favor projects with publicly available and positive audit reports.

- **Use Analytical Tools:** Leverage tools like BullX and PumpVision to independently verify the security of the smart contracts. These tools can provide detailed insights into contract behavior and potential risks.

Evaluating Tokenomics and Distribution

Fairness and Sustainability Assessed Through On-Chain Tracking of Large Holders

For Creators: Designing fair and sustainable tokenomics is essential for the long-term success of your meme coin.

- **Fair Distribution:** Ensure a fair distribution of tokens to avoid large concentrations of tokens held by a few individuals (whales). This promotes decentralization and reduces the risk of price manipulation.

- **Sustainable Supply:** Plan a sustainable token supply model, whether it's a fixed supply, inflationary, or deflationary mechanisms. Clearly communicate the tokenomics to your community.

For Investors: Understanding a meme coin's tokenomics is crucial for assessing its potential for growth and sustainability.

- **Analyze Distribution:** Use on-chain tracking tools to monitor the distribution of tokens. A balanced distribution with no significant concentration among a few wallets indicates a healthier project.

- **Evaluate Supply Mechanisms:** Assess the token supply model to determine if it supports long-term sustainability. Avoid projects with excessively high inflation rates or unclear supply mechanisms.

Assessing the Development Team

Background Checks, Verifying Dev Wallets That Launched Successful Tokens Previously

For Creators: Having a credible and experienced development team is key to building trust and ensuring the project's success.

- **Transparent Team Information:** Provide detailed information about the team members, including their backgrounds, expertise, and past projects. Transparency builds credibility and trust within the community.

- **Wallet Verification:** Verify that the development team's wallets have a history of launching successful tokens. This demonstrates their experience and commitment to the project.

For Investors: Evaluating the development team's credibility and experience can significantly influence your investment decisions.

- **Conduct Background Checks:** Research the team members' backgrounds to ensure they have the necessary expertise and a track record of successful projects. Look for verifiable information on LinkedIn, GitHub, and other professional platforms.

- **Verify Wallet Activity:** Use blockchain explorers and PumpVision to verify the development team's wallet activities. Check for past involvement in successful token launches and ensure there are no suspicious transactions.

Reviewing Social Media Presence

Activity and Engagement Measured with Tweet Trackers and Wallet-Based Influencer Tracking

For Creators: A strong social media presence is vital for promoting your meme coin and engaging with your community.

- **Active Engagement:** Regularly post updates, interact with followers, and respond to questions on platforms like Twitter (X), Instagram, TikTok, Discord, and Reddit. Consistent activity keeps your community informed and engaged.

- **Use Tweet Trackers:** Implement tweet trackers to monitor and analyze your social media performance. Tools like PumpVision can help you track engagement metrics, identify trending topics, and optimize your social media strategy.

For Investors: A robust social media presence can indicate a project's commitment to communication and community engagement.

- **Assess Activity Levels:** Check how active the project is on social media platforms. Frequent updates and active interactions suggest a dedicated team and a thriving community.

- **Monitor Engagement:** Use tweet trackers and wallet-based influencer tracking to evaluate the level of engagement and authenticity. High engagement rates and genuine interactions are positive indicators of a strong project.

Monitoring Community Sentiment

Gauging Positivity, Detecting Potential Scams via Social Signals and Unusual Wallet Activity

For Creators: Understanding community sentiment helps you address concerns, improve your project, and maintain a positive environment.

- **Sentiment Analysis:** Use tools like PumpVision to analyze the sentiment of community discussions. Positive sentiment indicates strong support, while negative sentiment can highlight areas needing attention.

- **Address Concerns Promptly:** Actively monitor feedback and address any issues or concerns raised by the community. Transparent and responsive communication fosters trust and loyalty.

For Investors: Monitoring community sentiment can provide early warnings about potential issues and help you make informed investment decisions.

- **Gauge Positivity:** Observe the overall mood of the community. A positive and supportive community is a good sign, while widespread negativity may indicate underlying problems.

- **Detect Scams:** Use social signals and monitor unusual wallet activity to identify potential scams. Sudden increases in token holders or large transfers can be red flags for pump-and-dump schemes or fraudulent activities.

Checking for Transparency and Communication

Regular Updates, Public Audits, and On-Chain Verifiable Proof of Marketing Expenses

For Creators: Transparency is a cornerstone of building trust with your community and investors.

- **Regular Updates:** Provide consistent and detailed updates about your project's progress, upcoming features, and any challenges you're facing. Use newsletters, blog posts, and social media to disseminate this information.

- **Public Audits:** Share the results of smart contract audits and other security assessments publicly. This demonstrates your commitment to security and builds credibility.

- **On-Chain Proof:** Use blockchain data to verify marketing expenses and other financial activities. Tools like PumpVision can help you provide verifiable proof of expenditures, ensuring transparency and accountability.

For Investors: Transparency from the development team is a key indicator of trustworthiness and reliability.

- **Review Updates:** Regularly check for updates from the project's team. Consistent communication shows that the team is actively working on the project and keeps the community informed.

- **Verify Audits:** Ensure that audit reports are publicly accessible and thoroughly review them to confirm that the smart contracts are secure.

- **Check On-Chain Proof:** Use blockchain explorers and PumpVision to verify the project's financial activities. Transparent proof of marketing expenses and other expenditures reduces the risk of hidden agendas or misuse of funds.

Identifying Red Flags for Potential Scams

Reused Twitter Handles, Copied Websites, Bundling Behavior (Multiple Related Wallets Buying in Sync)

For Creators: Maintaining a scam-free environment protects your project's reputation and ensures long-term success.

- **Secure Branding:** Avoid using reused or generic Twitter handles and ensure your website is original and professionally designed. Consistent and unique branding reduces the risk of being mistaken for a scam.

- **Monitor Wallet Activity:** Use tools like PumpVision to track wallet activities and detect any suspicious patterns, such as multiple related wallets buying tokens in sync. This can help prevent pump-and-dump schemes and other fraudulent activities.

For Investors: Recognizing red flags is essential to avoid falling victim to scams and fraudulent projects.

- **Check Social Media Handles:** Verify that the project's social media handles are official and not reused by scammers. Look for consistency in branding and authenticity in interactions.

- **Inspect Websites:** Ensure that the project's website is original, well-designed, and free from copied content. Scam websites often have poor design quality and may contain plagiarized material from legitimate projects.

- **Analyze Wallet Behavior:** Use blockchain explorers and PumpVision to monitor wallet activities. Be wary of projects where multiple wallets are purchasing tokens simultaneously, as this can indicate coordinated pump-and-dump schemes.

Running Discord Commands to Check Suspicious Username Reuse or Website Similarity

For Creators: Protect your community by actively monitoring for potential impersonations or scams.

- **Use Discord Bots:** Implement bots that can scan for suspicious username reuse or detect websites that closely resemble your official site. These bots can automatically flag or remove suspicious accounts, maintaining a safe environment for your community.

- **Educate Your Community:** Inform your community members about common scam tactics and encourage them to verify official channels before engaging or investing.

For Investors: Stay vigilant and use available tools to verify the legitimacy of the projects you're interested in.

- **Use Verification Tools:** Utilize Discord commands and bots to check for suspicious activity within community channels. This can help you identify impersonators or malicious users trying to scam community members.

- **Verify Official Sources:** Always cross-check information from multiple official channels to ensure you're interacting with legitimate representatives of the project.

Using Analytical Tools and Platforms

Pump.fun, CoinGecko, BirdEye, Cielo for Real-Time Data on New Launches and Wallet Activities

For Creators: Leverage analytical tools to gain insights into your project's performance and optimize your strategies.

- **Pump.fun:** Utilize Pump.fun's suite of tools for token creation, liquidity management, and marketing automation. Its integration with PumpVision provides comprehensive analytics and monitoring capabilities.

- **CoinGecko and Other Platforms:** List your meme coin on platforms like CoinGecko to gain visibility and track performance metrics. These platforms offer detailed data on trading volumes, market capitalization, and price trends.

- **BirdEye and Cielo:** Use BirdEye for sentiment analysis and community engagement tracking. Cielo can provide advanced wallet activity insights, helping you understand how users are interacting with your token.

For Investors: Analytical tools are indispensable for conducting due diligence and making informed investment decisions.

- **Real-Time Data:** Use platforms like CoinGecko and Pump.fun to access real-time data on new meme coin launches, trading volumes, and price movements. This helps you stay updated on the latest market trends and identify promising projects early.

- **Wallet Activity Tracking:** Tools like Cielo allow you to monitor wallet activities, helping you identify patterns that indicate healthy project growth or potential red flags for scams.

- **Sentiment Analysis:** BirdEye can provide insights into community sentiment, allowing you to gauge the overall positivity or negativity surrounding a project. Positive sentiment is often a good indicator of community support and project viability.

Making Informed Investment Decisions

Balancing Potential Rewards with Verified Security Checks and Historical On-Chain Data

For Creators: Providing clear and comprehensive information to investors fosters trust and encourages investment.

- **Transparent Reporting:** Share detailed reports on tokenomics, development progress, and liquidity management. Use on-chain data to back your claims and provide verifiable proof of your project's health.

- **Educate Your Community:** Help investors understand the key indicators of success by providing educational content and resources. This empowers them to make informed decisions and increases their confidence in your project.

For Investors: Making informed investment decisions requires a balanced approach that considers both the potential rewards and the associated risks.

- **Assess Key Indicators:** Evaluate community size, liquidity, development activity, and social media presence to gauge the project's potential for success. Use analytical tools to verify these indicators through blockchain explorers and PumpVision.

- **Verify Security:** Ensure that the meme coin's smart contracts are secure and have undergone thorough audits. Use tools like BullX and PumpVision to analyze code integrity and detect any vulnerabilities.

- **Analyze Tokenomics:** Review the token distribution and supply mechanisms to ensure fairness and sustainability. Use on-chain tracking to monitor large holders and avoid projects with concentrated token distributions that could lead to manipulation.

- **Evaluate the Team:** Conduct background checks on the development team and verify their past performance. Ensure that the team has a history of successful projects and that their wallets reflect genuine support for the meme coin.

- **Monitor Community Sentiment:** Use social signals and sentiment analysis tools to gauge the community's positivity and support for the project. Positive community sentiment is a strong indicator of a meme coin's potential for growth and stability.

- **Check for Transparency:** Look for regular updates, public audits, and on-chain verifiable proof of marketing expenses. Transparency from the project's team is a key indicator of their commitment and reliability.

- **Identify Red Flags:** Be cautious of projects with reused social media handles, copied websites, or suspicious wallet activities. Use analytical tools to detect potential scams and avoid investing in high-risk projects.

- **Use Comprehensive Tools:** Leverage platforms like Pump.fun , CoinGecko, BirdEye, and Cielo to access real-time data, track wallet activities, and monitor community sentiment. These tools provide the insights needed to make data-driven investment decisions.

Identifying key indicators of success for meme coins is essential for both creators aiming to build a thriving project and investors seeking lucrative opportunities. By focusing on community size, liquidity, development activity, smart contract security, tokenomics, team credibility, social media presence, community sentiment, transparency, and vigilance against scams, you can navigate the meme coin landscape with greater confidence and insight.

For creators, leveraging tools like Pump.fun and PumpVision can streamline the process of creating, managing, and promoting your meme coin, ensuring that your project stands out in a crowded market. By maintaining transparency, fostering a strong community, and continuously monitoring and improving your project's health, you lay the foundation for long-term success and sustainability.

For investors, understanding and analyzing these key indicators equips you with the knowledge needed to make informed decisions and mitigate risks. Utilizing analytical platforms and blockchain data, conducting thorough due diligence, and staying vigilant against red flags will help you identify legitimate and promising meme coins amidst the many projects vying for attention.

In the dynamic and rapidly evolving world of cryptocurrencies, staying informed and leveraging the right tools and strategies is crucial. Whether you're a creator looking to launch a successful meme coin or an investor seeking the next big opportunity, understanding these key indicators of success will empower you to navigate the crypto landscape effectively and achieve your goals.

By following the comprehensive guidelines outlined in this guide, both creators and investors can enhance their understanding of what makes a meme coin successful, ensuring that their efforts and investments are well-placed in the pursuit of cryptocurrency excellence.

Chapter 8
Buying and Managing Your Meme Coin Investments

Venturing into the world of meme coins can be both exciting and overwhelming, especially for beginners. One of the crucial steps in this journey is setting up on a cryptocurrency exchange. Exchanges serve as the primary platforms where you can buy, sell, and trade your meme coins. This comprehensive guide will walk you through each step, focusing on the use of Pump.fun, a powerful tool for managing your meme coin activities, while also incorporating other essential platforms and tools to ensure a smooth and secure experience.

Creating Accounts on Reputable Exchanges and Confirming Token Authenticity On-Chain

Choosing the Right Exchange

Before you can trade your meme coins, you need to choose a reputable cryptocurrency exchange. Reputable exchanges are those that are secure, have a large user base, offer a variety of trading pairs, and comply with regulatory standards. Some of the most well-known exchanges include:

- **Binance:** One of the largest and most popular exchanges globally, offering a wide range of cryptocurrencies and trading pairs.

- **Coinbase:** Known for its user-friendly interface, making it ideal for beginners.

- **Kraken:** Offers advanced trading features and strong security measures.

- **Uniswap:** A decentralized exchange (DEX) popular for trading Ethereum-based tokens.

- **PancakeSwap:** A DEX on the Binance Smart Chain, ideal for BEP-20 tokens.

Creating Your Exchange Account

1. **Sign Up:**

   ◦ Visit the official website of your chosen exchange (e.g., Binance, Coinbase).

   ◦ Click on the "Sign Up" or "Register" button.

   ◦ Enter your email address and create a strong password. Ensure your password is unique and not used for any other accounts.

2. **Verification:**

   ◦ Complete the Know Your Customer (KYC) process. This typically involves uploading identification documents such as a passport or driver's license and a proof of address (e.g., utility bill).

   ◦ Follow the exchange's instructions to verify your identity. This step is crucial for unlocking higher trading limits and ensuring the security of your account.

3. **Secure Your Account:**

   ◦ Enable Two-Factor Authentication (2FA) using an app like Google Authenticator or Authy. This adds an extra layer of security to protect your account from unauthorized access.

Confirming Token Authenticity On-Chain

Once your account is set up, it's essential to confirm the authenticity of the meme coin you intend to trade. This ensures you're dealing with a legitimate token and not a scam.

1. **Obtain the Token Contract Address:**

   - Use Pump.fun to generate your meme coin or get the contract address if you're investing in one.

   - Ensure you copy the exact contract address, as sending funds to an incorrect address can result in permanent loss.

2. **Verify on Blockchain Explorers:**

   - Use blockchain explorers like Etherscan for Ethereum-based tokens or BscScan for Binance Smart Chain tokens.

   - Paste the token contract address into the search bar.

   - Check for details such as the token name, symbol, total supply, and transaction history. Look for verified contracts marked with a checkmark, indicating they have been audited and are genuine.

3. **Cross-Reference with Pump.fun:**

   - Use Pump.fun's PumpVision tool to analyze the token's on-chain data. This tool can provide insights into liquidity, large holder distributions, and overall token activity.

   - Ensure that the token's data matches the information provided by the exchange and the blockchain explorer.

Funding Your Exchange Account

To start trading, you need to fund your exchange account. This can be done by depositing fiat currency (like USD, EUR) or cryptocurrencies.

Depositing Fiat Currency

1. **Navigate to the Deposit Section:**

   - Once logged in, go to the "Wallet" or "Funds" section of the exchange.

   - Select "Deposit" and choose your preferred fiat currency.

2. **Choose a Payment Method:**

   - Exchanges typically offer multiple payment options such as bank transfers, credit/debit cards, or third-party payment processors.

   - Select the method that is most convenient for you.

3. **Complete the Deposit:**

   - Follow the instructions to complete the deposit. This may involve providing bank details or entering credit card information.

   - Be aware of any fees associated with the deposit method you choose.

Depositing Cryptocurrency

1. **Select Cryptocurrency:**

   - In the "Deposit" section, choose the cryptocurrency you wish to deposit (e.g., Bitcoin, Ethereum).

   - Copy the deposit address provided by the exchange.

2. **Transfer Funds from Your Wallet:**

- Open your personal wallet (e.g., MetaMask, Trust Wallet) where your cryptocurrency is stored.

- Initiate a transfer by entering the exchange's deposit address and specifying the amount to send.

- Confirm the transaction and wait for it to be processed. This can take anywhere from a few minutes to several hours, depending on the network congestion.

Verifying Wallet Ownership and Transaction Histories

To ensure the security and legitimacy of your investments, verifying wallet ownership and transaction histories is crucial.

1. **Verify Your Wallet:**

- Some exchanges may require you to verify the wallet you're depositing from. This involves proving ownership by signing a message or completing a small test transaction.

- Follow the exchange's instructions to complete the verification process.

2. **Review Transaction History:**

- Use blockchain explorers and PumpVision to review your transaction history. Ensure all past transactions are legitimate and that your wallet hasn't been involved in any suspicious activities.

- This step helps protect you from potential security threats and ensures that your funds are safe.

Placing Buy Orders: Market vs. Limit Orders

Once your exchange account is funded, you can place buy orders to acquire meme coins. Understanding the difference between market and limit orders is essential for effective trading.

Market Orders

A market order is a request to buy a cryptocurrency immediately at the current market price.

Advantages:

- **Speed:** Executes instantly, ensuring you get into a trade quickly.

- **Simplicity:** Easy to place without needing to set specific price points.

Disadvantages:

- **Price Uncertainty:** The exact price at which the order will execute is not guaranteed, especially in volatile markets.

How to Place a Market Order:

1. **Navigate to the Trading Section:** Go to the exchange's trading or markets page.

2. **Select the Trading Pair:** Choose the pair you want to trade (e.g., MEME/USD).

3. **Choose Market Order:** Select the market order option.

4. **Enter the Amount:** Specify how much you want to buy.

5. **Confirm the Order:** Review the details and confirm the purchase.

Limit Orders

A limit order allows you to buy a cryptocurrency at a specific price or better.

Advantages:

- **Price Control:** Ensures you buy at your desired price or lower.

- **Potential Savings:** Can save money if the market price drops to your limit price.

Disadvantages:

- **Execution Risk:** The order may not execute if the market price doesn't reach your limit price.

How to Place a Limit Order:

1. **Navigate to the Trading Section:** Access the exchange's trading or markets page.

2. **Select the Trading Pair:** Choose the pair you want to trade (e.g., MEME/USD).

3. **Choose Limit Order:** Select the limit order option.

4. **Set the Price:** Enter the price at which you want to buy the token.

5. **Enter the Amount:** Specify how much you want to buy.

6. **Confirm the Order:** Review the details and place the limit order.

Leveraging Specialized Tools to Find the Best Entry Points

Utilizing tools like PumpVision can help you analyze market trends and identify the best times to place your orders.

- **Chart Analysis:** Use PumpVision's integrated charting tools to analyze historical price data and identify patterns.

- **Technical Indicators:** Apply indicators like Moving Averages (MA), Relative Strength Index (RSI), and Bollinger Bands to gauge market momentum and potential reversal points.

- **Real-Time Alerts:** Set up real-time alerts for price movements or indicator triggers to stay informed about optimal entry points.

Securing Your Investments: Hardware Wallets and Verified Contract Addresses

Security is paramount when dealing with cryptocurrencies. Protecting your investments involves using secure wallets and ensuring the tokens you hold are legitimate.

Hardware Wallets

Hardware wallets are physical devices that store your cryptocurrency offline, providing enhanced security against hacking and theft.

Popular Hardware Wallets:

- **Ledger Nano S/X:** Offers robust security features and supports a wide range of cryptocurrencies.

- **Trezor Model T:** Known for its user-friendly interface and strong security protocols.

How to Use a Hardware Wallet:

1. **Purchase from Official Sources:** Buy hardware wallets directly from the manufacturer or authorized retailers to avoid counterfeit devices.

2. **Set Up the Wallet:** Follow the manufacturer's instructions to initialize the device. This typically involves setting up a PIN and writing down a seed phrase (a series of words that can be used to recover

your wallet).

3. **Transfer Tokens:** Connect your hardware wallet to your computer or mobile device using the provided USB or Bluetooth connection. Use the wallet's interface to transfer your meme coins from the exchange to your hardware wallet's address.

Ensuring Tokens Match Verified Contract Addresses

To avoid scams and ensure you're holding genuine tokens, always verify that the tokens in your wallet match the verified contract addresses.

1. **Check Contract Address:**

   - Use Pump.fun's PumpVision to verify the token's contract address.

   - Cross-reference with blockchain explorers like Etherscan or BscScan.

2. **Confirm Token Details:**

   - Ensure the token name, symbol, and total supply match the official information provided by the project.

3. **Use Verified Listings:**

   - Only interact with tokens listed on reputable exchanges and verified by tools like PumpVision. Avoid tokens with mismatched or suspicious contract addresses.

Monitoring Market Trends and Price Movements

Staying informed about market trends and price movements is essential for making timely and profitable trading decisions. Utilizing charts, indicators, and real-time blockchain feeds can provide valuable insights into the market's behavior.

Using Charts and Technical Indicators

Charts and technical indicators are fundamental tools for analyzing market trends and predicting future price movements.

Popular Chart Types:

- **Candlestick Charts:** Show price movements over time, highlighting open, high, low, and close prices within a specific period.

- **Line Charts:** Display a simple line representing the closing prices over time.

Key Technical Indicators:

- **Moving Averages (MA):** Smooth out price data to identify trends over specific periods (e.g., 50-day MA, 200-day MA).

- **Relative Strength Index (RSI):** Measures the speed and change of price movements to identify overbought or oversold conditions.

- **Bollinger Bands:** Indicate volatility by showing the upper and lower bands around a moving average.

How to Use Pump.fun's PumpVision for Chart Analysis

1. **Access PumpVision:** Log in to your Pump.fun account and navigate to the PumpVision dashboard.

2. **Select the Token:** Choose your meme coin from the list of available

tokens.

3. **Analyze the Charts:** Use PumpVision's charting tools to apply technical indicators and analyze price trends.

4. **Identify Patterns:** Look for patterns such as head and shoulders, double tops/bottoms, and trend lines to predict potential price movements.

Real-Time Blockchain Feeds

Real-time blockchain feeds provide up-to-the-minute data on transactions and other on-chain activities, offering deeper insights into market dynamics.

Benefits of Real-Time Feeds:

- **Immediate Updates:** Stay informed about new transactions, large transfers, and other significant activities as they happen.

- **Enhanced Transparency:** Gain a clear view of token distribution and movement within the network.

Using Pump.fun's PumpVision for Real-Time Insights:

- **Transaction Monitoring:** Track large transactions and unusual wallet activities that could impact the token's price.

- **Liquidity Tracking:** Monitor the liquidity pools on various DEXs to ensure there is sufficient support for trading activities.

- **Alert System:** Set up custom alerts for specific events, such as sudden spikes in trading volume or large token transfers.

Implementing Risk Management Strategies

Effective risk management is crucial to protect your investments and maximize potential returns. Implementing strategies like diversification, stop-loss orders, and tracking insider wallets can help mitigate risks associated with meme coin trading.

Diversification

Diversification involves spreading your investments across multiple assets to reduce exposure to any single asset's risk.

For Creators:

- **Token Variety:** Offer multiple token types or utility tokens within your ecosystem to diversify revenue streams and reduce dependency on a single token.

- **Market Expansion:** Expand your meme coin's presence across different blockchain networks and exchanges to reach a broader audience and mitigate risks associated with platform-specific issues.

For Investors:

- **Portfolio Spread:** Invest in a variety of meme coins and other cryptocurrencies to minimize the impact of poor performance in any single asset.

- **Balanced Allocation:** Allocate your investment capital across different asset classes, including stablecoins and high-risk meme coins, to balance potential rewards with risk exposure.

Stop-Loss Orders

Stop-loss orders are predefined sell orders that trigger when a token's price reaches a specific level, limiting potential losses.

How to Set Stop-Loss Orders:

1. **Determine the Stop-Loss Price:** Decide the maximum amount you're willing to lose on a trade (e.g., 10% below your purchase price).

2. **Place the Order:** On your exchange, select the stop-loss order option and enter the stop price.

3. **Automatic Execution:** If the token's price falls to the stop price, the stop-loss order will automatically sell your tokens, preventing further losses.

Using Pump.fun's PumpVision:

- **Automated Alerts:** Set up alerts to notify you when a token's price approaches your stop-loss level.

- **Integration with Trading Bots:** Use PumpVision to integrate with trading bots that can automatically execute stop-loss orders based on your predefined criteria.

Tracking Insider Wallets to Avoid Pump-and-Dumps

Insider wallets are those controlled by the project's creators or large holders (whales) who can significantly influence the token's price.

For Creators:

- **Transparent Token Distribution:** Ensure that a fair distribution model is in place to prevent large holders from manipulating the market.

- **Community Monitoring:** Use PumpVision to monitor insider wallet activities and maintain transparency with your community about large transactions.

For Investors:

- **Monitor Large Transactions:** Use blockchain explorers and PumpVision to track transactions from insider wallets. Large buy or sell orders from these wallets can indicate potential pump-and-dump schemes.

- **Assess Whale Activity:** Evaluate the trading patterns of large holders to determine if they are supporting the token's growth or attempting to manipulate its price.

Staying Informed with Market News

Staying updated with the latest market news is essential for making informed trading decisions. Following crypto news and using tweet trackers can help you stay ahead of influential announcements and market-moving events.

Following Crypto News

Regularly consuming crypto news ensures you're aware of the latest developments, regulatory changes, and market trends that can impact your investments.

Popular Crypto News Sources:

- **CoinDesk:** Offers in-depth news, analysis, and research on cryptocurrency and blockchain technology.

- **CoinTelegraph:** Provides breaking news, expert opinions, and market updates.

- **CryptoSlate:** Features news, data, and analysis on a wide range of crypto projects and trends.

Using Pump.fun's PumpVision:

- **News Aggregation:** Access curated crypto news directly within PumpVision to stay informed without switching platforms.

- **Custom News Feeds:** Set up personalized news feeds based on your interests and the specific meme coins you're tracking.

Using Tweet Trackers to Detect Influential Announcements

Tweet trackers are tools that monitor specific Twitter accounts for new tweets and notify you in real-time. These trackers are invaluable for catching influential announcements that can impact a token's price.

How to Use Tweet Trackers:

1. **Select Key Accounts:** Choose influential accounts related to your meme coins, such as project founders, major investors, and trusted crypto analysts.

2. **Set Up Notifications:** Use PumpVision to set up real-time notifications whenever these accounts tweet about your meme coins.

3. **Stay Updated:** Receive instant alerts on your phone or computer, ensuring you never miss crucial updates or market-moving news.

Benefits for Investors:

- **Timely Information:** Get immediate access to important announcements, such as partnership deals, exchange listings, or significant project milestones.

- **Informed Trading:** Use the information from tweet trackers to make timely buy or sell decisions based on the latest developments.

Engaging with the Project's Community

Active participation in the project's community can provide deeper insights and validate the project's claims. Engaging with the community also fosters a sense of ownership and trust.

Participating in Governance

Some meme coins offer governance features, allowing holders to vote on key decisions affecting the project's future.

How to Participate:

1. **Hold Tokens:** Ensure you hold a minimum amount of the meme coin to be eligible for voting.

2. **Join Governance Platforms:** Use platforms integrated with Pump.fun, like PumpVision, to access governance proposals and voting mechanisms.

3. **Cast Your Vote:** Participate in decision-making processes by voting on proposals that align with your vision for the project.

Benefits for Creators:

- **Community Input:** Gather valuable feedback and ideas from your community to guide project development.

- **Enhanced Trust:** Demonstrating a commitment to decentralized governance builds trust and loyalty among your community members.

Validating Project Claims On-Chain

Validating claims made by the project ensures that the information is accurate and transparent.

How to Validate Claims:

1. **On-Chain Verification:** Use PumpVision and blockchain explorers to verify claims related to token distribution, liquidity, and development progress.

2. **Smart Contract Analysis:** Review the smart contract's code and transaction history to ensure it aligns with the project's stated objectives.

3. **Audit Reports:** Check for publicly available audit reports and verify their authenticity using PumpVision's verification tools.

Benefits for Investors:

- **Informed Decisions:** Validate the project's claims to ensure they are legitimate and not exaggerated or false.

- **Reduced Risk:** Mitigate the risk of investing in projects with misleading or fraudulent information.

Rebalancing Your Portfolio

Rebalancing involves adjusting your investment holdings to maintain a desired level of risk and reward. This strategy ensures that your portfolio remains aligned with your financial goals and market conditions.

Adjusting Holdings Based on Performance

1. **Evaluate Performance:**

   - Regularly assess the performance of your meme coins using PumpVision's performance metrics.

   - Identify tokens that have underperformed or exceeded your expectations.

2. **Reallocate Funds:**

   - Sell a portion of underperforming tokens to reduce exposure and lock in any remaining value.

   - Invest in high-performing tokens or diversify into new meme coins to capitalize on growth opportunities.

3. **Maintain Balance:**

   ○ Ensure your portfolio remains diversified across different meme coins and other cryptocurrencies to spread risk and enhance potential returns.

Influenced by Verified Market Signals

Use verified market signals from tools like PumpVision to inform your rebalancing decisions.

- **Technical Indicators:** Utilize indicators such as Moving Averages (MA), RSI, and MACD to identify trends and potential reversal points.

- **On-Chain Data:** Leverage on-chain metrics like transaction volumes, active addresses, and liquidity levels to gauge market sentiment and token health.

- **Community Sentiment:** Monitor community discussions and sentiment to understand the broader perception of each meme coin in your portfolio.

Preparing for Exit Strategies

Knowing when and how to exit your investments is as important as knowing when to enter. Proper exit strategies help you maximize profits and minimize losses.

Knowing When and How to Sell

1. **Set Profit Targets:**

   ○ Define specific price points at which you plan to take profits. For example, you might decide to sell a portion of your holdings when the price increases by 50%.

2. **Implement Stop-Loss Orders:**

   ○ Protect your investments by setting stop-loss orders at predetermined price levels. This ensures you automatically sell your tokens if the price drops to a certain level, limiting potential losses.

3. **Monitor Market Conditions:**

   ○ Stay informed about market trends, news, and sentiment using PumpVision. Adjust your exit strategies based on changing market conditions and project developments.

Verifying Liquidity and Trading Volume Before Exiting

Before exiting your investment, ensure that the token has sufficient liquidity and trading volume to facilitate smooth transactions.

1. **Check Liquidity Levels:**

   ○ Use PumpVision to verify that the liquidity pools on your chosen exchanges are sufficient to handle large sell orders without causing significant price slippage.

2. **Analyze Trading Volume:**

   ○ Ensure there is consistent trading volume to facilitate easy buying and selling. Low trading volumes can result in difficulty exiting positions at desired price levels.

3. **Assess Exchange Health:**

   ○ Verify that the exchanges you're using are reputable and secure. Ensure that they have a good track record of handling large transactions smoothly.

Setting up on a cryptocurrency exchange is a fundamental step in trading and investing in meme coins. By following this comprehensive guide, beginners can navigate the complexities of exchange setups, secure their investments, and implement effective trading strategies. Utilizing tools like Pump.fun and PumpVision enhances your ability to make informed decisions, monitor market trends, and manage risks effectively. Whether you're a creator looking to list your meme coin or an investor aiming to maximize returns, understanding these key aspects ensures a smoother and more secure cryptocurrency journey.

Chapter 9
Pumping Your Meme Coin Ethically

Launching a meme coin can be an exhilarating venture, filled with the potential for rapid growth and widespread recognition. However, with great opportunity comes great responsibility. One of the most critical aspects of ensuring your meme coin's success lies in how you promote it. This chapter, "Pumping Your Meme Coin Ethically," delves into the nuances of creating genuine hype without resorting to manipulative or unethical practices. We will explore how to leverage Pump.fun and other tools to build a trustworthy and sustainable project, ensuring long-term success and community trust.

Understanding the Concept of "Pumping"

What Does "Pumping" Mean?

In the cryptocurrency world, "pumping" refers to the act of artificially inflating the price of a token through coordinated buying, aggressive marketing, or spreading positive news. While this can create short-term excitement and increase a token's visibility, it often attracts scrutiny and can lead to unsustainable price bubbles or pump-and-dump schemes.

Differentiating Ethical Promotion from Manipulative Schemes

Ethical promotion focuses on building genuine interest and trust in your meme coin through transparent and honest marketing efforts. In contrast, manipulative schemes involve misleading tactics to create artificial demand, often leading to rapid price increases followed by sharp declines once the manipulation ceases.

Ethical Promotion:

- **Transparency:** Clearly communicate your project's goals, tokenomics, and development progress.

- **Honesty:** Avoid making exaggerated claims or promising unrealistic returns.

- **Community Engagement:** Foster a supportive and active community through genuine interactions and value-driven content.

Manipulative Schemes:

- **False Hype:** Spreading unverified or false information to inflate interest.

- **Coordinated Buying:** Pumping the token's price through coordinated buying without underlying value.

- **Pump-and-Dump:** Selling off tokens at inflated prices, causing the price to crash and leaving investors with losses.

Building Genuine Hype Through Quality Content

Creating Engaging, Valuable Content That Resounds with Verified Trends

Quality content is the cornerstone of ethical promotion. It involves creating informative, entertaining, and valuable materials that resonate with your target audience and align with current trends.

Steps to Create Quality Content:

1. **Identify Trends:** Use tools like Pump.fun's PumpVision to identify trending topics and themes within the crypto and meme communities.

2. **Content Variety:** Develop a mix of content types, including blog posts, videos, infographics, and memes that cater to different preferences.

3. **Educational Value:** Provide educational content that helps your community understand your meme coin's unique features, use cases, and benefits.

4. **Engagement:** Encourage interaction by asking questions, hosting polls, and inviting feedback. Respond promptly to comments and messages to build a sense of community.

Example Content Ideas:

- **Explainer Videos:** Short videos explaining the purpose and mechanics of your meme coin.

- **Behind-the-Scenes Posts:** Share insights into the development process and team activities.

- **Community Spotlights:** Highlight active community members and their contributions.

Leveraging Social Media Platforms Effectively

Using Tweet Trackers and Front-Running Influencer Announcements Ethically

Social media platforms are powerful tools for promoting your meme coin. When used ethically, they can significantly boost your project's visibility and credibility.

Effective Use of Social Media:

1. **Consistent Branding:** Ensure your social media profiles reflect your meme coin's branding, including logos, color schemes, and messaging.

2. **Engagement Strategies:** Regularly post updates, respond to comments, and engage with your followers to maintain an active and vibrant community.

3. **Tweet Trackers:** Utilize tools like Pump.fun's PumpVision to set up tweet trackers that notify your community about important announcements. This ensures timely dissemination of information without overwhelming users.

4. **Ethical Front-Running:** If collaborating with influencers, ensure that announcements and promotions are genuine and not timed solely to manipulate the market. Avoid orchestrating coordinated buy orders around influencer posts.

Best Practices:

- **Authentic Interactions:** Engage with your community authentically. Share your journey, celebrate milestones, and acknowledge community contributions.

- **Avoid Spam:** Refrain from spamming your followers with excessive posts. Focus on quality over quantity.

- **Use Verified Accounts:** Promote your meme coin through verified and reputable social media accounts to enhance credibility.

Organizing Community Events and Giveaways

Incentivizing Engagement with Verifiable Airdrops and On-Chain Proof of Fairness

Community events and giveaways are excellent ways to foster engagement and reward loyal supporters. When conducted ethically, they can enhance community trust and participation.

Types of Community Incentives:

1. **Airdrops:** Distribute free tokens to community members. Use Pump.fun to manage and verify airdrop eligibility, ensuring fairness and transparency.

2. **Staking Rewards:** Offer rewards for staking tokens, encouraging long-term holding and participation.

3. **Referral Programs:** Incentivize members to refer new investors by rewarding both the referrer and the referred.

Ensuring Fairness:

- **Transparent Criteria:** Clearly outline the criteria for participation in giveaways and airdrops.

- **On-Chain Proof:** Use blockchain data to verify that rewards are distributed fairly and as promised. Tools like PumpVision can help track and confirm distribution.

- **Audit Trails:** Maintain records of all giveaways and airdrops, allowing community members to verify the fairness and integrity of the process.

Example Event Ideas:

- **Memes Contests:** Encourage the creation and sharing of memes related to your project, rewarding the best entries with tokens.

- **AMA Sessions:** Host Ask Me Anything sessions where the team answers questions and engages directly with the community.

- **Virtual Meetups:** Organize virtual events where community members can connect, share ideas, and celebrate milestones together.

Collaborating with Influencers and Content Creators

Partnering with Influencers Who Have Transparent, Profitable On-Chain Histories

Influencer partnerships can amplify your meme coin's reach and credibility when approached ethically. Selecting the right influencers who have a proven track record of supporting legitimate projects is crucial.

Steps to Collaborate with Influencers:

1. **Identify Authentic Influencers:** Use Pump.fun's PumpVision to verify the authenticity of influencers by checking their on-chain histories and past collaborations.

2. **Evaluate Past Performance:** Review the influencer's previous partnerships and their impact on those projects. Look for evidence of successful promotions and genuine engagement.

3. **Transparent Agreements:** Clearly outline the terms of collaboration, ensuring that influencers disclose any sponsorships or partnerships transparently to their audiences.

4. **Genuine Endorsements:** Encourage influencers to share honest opinions about your meme coin, highlighting its unique features and

potential without making exaggerated claims.

Benefits of Authentic Influencer Partnerships:

- **Increased Visibility:** Reach a broader audience through the influencer's established follower base.

- **Enhanced Credibility:** Leverage the trust and authority that influencers have built with their audiences.

- **Community Growth:** Attract new community members who trust the influencer's recommendations.

Best Practices:

- **Long-Term Relationships:** Build long-term partnerships with influencers who genuinely support your project.

- **Diverse Collaborations:** Collaborate with a variety of influencers across different platforms to maximize reach and engagement.

- **Monitor Performance:** Use analytics tools to track the effectiveness of influencer campaigns and adjust strategies as needed.

Utilizing Paid Advertising Responsibly

Targeted Ads Without Misleading Information and Verifiable ROI

Paid advertising can significantly boost your meme coin's visibility and attract new investors. However, it's essential to use advertising responsibly to maintain trust and integrity.

Strategies for Responsible Paid Advertising:

1. **Targeted Campaigns:** Use platforms like Google Ads, Facebook Ads, and crypto-specific ad networks to target your ads to specific demo-

graphics interested in cryptocurrency and meme culture.

2. **Clear Messaging:** Ensure your ads communicate your meme coin's unique value proposition clearly and honestly. Avoid misleading claims or exaggerated promises.

3. **Verifiable ROI:** Track the return on investment (ROI) of your ad campaigns using tools like Pump.fun's PumpVision. Analyze metrics such as click-through rates, conversion rates, and overall engagement to assess the effectiveness of your campaigns.

4. **Compliance:** Adhere to advertising regulations and guidelines set by each platform. This includes avoiding unsubstantiated claims and ensuring transparency in sponsored content.

Best Practices:

- **A/B Testing:** Experiment with different ad creatives and messages to identify what resonates best with your target audience.

- **Budget Management:** Allocate your advertising budget wisely, focusing on channels and strategies that yield the highest ROI.

- **Continuous Optimization:** Regularly review and optimize your ad campaigns based on performance data to maximize effectiveness and minimize costs.

Ethical Considerations:

- **Avoid Pump-and-Dump Tactics:** Do not use ads to create false hype or manipulate the market. Focus on genuine value propositions and long-term growth.

- **Transparency in Sponsorships:** Clearly disclose any sponsored content or partnerships to maintain transparency and trust with your audience.

Creating Viral Marketing Campaigns

Strategically Encouraging Organic Sharing While Providing Blockchain-Proofed Legitimacy

Viral marketing campaigns can exponentially increase your meme coin's visibility and attract a massive influx of new investors. However, achieving virality ethically requires strategic planning and authentic engagement.

Steps to Create Viral Campaigns:

1. **Leverage Current Trends:** Use tools like Pump.fun's PumpVision to identify and capitalize on trending topics and memes within the crypto and broader internet culture.

2. **Create Shareable Content:** Develop engaging and entertaining content that encourages users to share with their networks. This includes memes, short videos, and interactive posts.

3. **Incentivize Sharing:** Offer rewards for users who help spread the word about your meme coin. This could include referral bonuses, exclusive access to events, or additional token rewards.

4. **Blockchain-Proofed Legitimacy:**

Creating Viral Marketing Campaigns

Incorporate on-chain data and transparency into your viral campaigns to enhance credibility and trust. By demonstrating that your promotional efforts are backed by verifiable blockchain activity, you can differentiate your meme coin from others and build a more trustworthy image.

How to Implement Blockchain-Proofed Legitimacy:

- **Share Transaction Proofs:** Highlight significant transactions, such as large buy orders or liquidity additions, on your social media platforms. Use PumpVision to provide real-time data that verifies these actions.

- **Transparent Campaign Tracking:** Utilize tools like Pump.fun to track the success of your viral campaigns. Share metrics and insights with your community to show the genuine impact of your marketing efforts.

- **Public Smart Contracts:** Ensure that any smart contracts associated with your viral campaigns, such as those used for airdrops or giveaways, are publicly accessible and verifiable. This transparency reassures participants that the campaigns are fair and legitimate.

Example Viral Campaign Ideas:

- **Meme Contests:** Host contests where participants create and share memes related to your meme coin. Offer rewards for the most creative and widely shared memes.

- **Influencer Challenges:** Collaborate with influencers to create challenges that encourage their followers to engage with your meme coin. For example, a dance or art challenge that incorporates your token's branding.

- **Interactive Games:** Develop simple games or quizzes that educate users about your meme coin while encouraging them to share their results on social media.

Maintaining Transparency During Promotions

Publishing Verifiable Wallet Addresses and Transaction Proofs

Transparency is a key factor in building trust with your community and investors. By providing verifiable proof of your token's activities and financial transactions, you can enhance your meme coin's credibility and differentiate it from fraudulent projects.

Steps to Maintain Transparency:

1. **Publish Wallet Addresses:**

   ○ Share the official wallet addresses used for liquidity pools, marketing funds, and development activities. Ensure these addresses are prominently displayed on your website and social media profiles.

2. **Provide Transaction Proofs:**

   ○ Regularly share transaction proofs for significant activities, such as liquidity additions, airdrops, and staking rewards. Use blockchain explorers and PumpVision to generate and share these proofs.

3. **Public Audits:**

   ○ Conduct and publish regular audits of your smart contracts and financial transactions. Share audit reports and summaries with your community to demonstrate ongoing commitment to security and transparency.

4. **Transparent Marketing Expenses:**

   ○ Use on-chain tracking tools like PumpVision to verify and publish your marketing expenses. This includes detailing how funds are allocated and spent, ensuring that your marketing efforts are legitimate and not misleading.

Benefits of Transparency:

• **Builds Trust:** Transparent practices reassure investors and community members that the project is legitimate and well-managed.

• **Prevents Scams:** By openly sharing wallet addresses and transaction data, you make it difficult for scammers to impersonate your project or manipulate its tokenomics.

- **Enhances Reputation:** Transparency fosters a positive reputation within the crypto community, attracting more genuine investors and supporters.

Measuring the Impact of Your Promotional Efforts

Using Analytics and Blockchain Data to Assess Effectiveness

To ensure your promotional efforts are yielding positive results, it's essential to measure their impact using analytics and blockchain data. This allows you to understand what strategies are working, identify areas for improvement, and make data-driven decisions to optimize your marketing efforts.

Key Metrics to Track:

1. **Engagement Rates:**

   - Measure likes, shares, comments, and overall interaction with your social media posts and content. High engagement rates indicate that your content is resonating with your audience.

2. **Conversion Rates:**

   - Track how many people are converting from viewers to active community members or token holders. This can be measured through website analytics, social media insights, and on-chain data.

3. **Traffic Sources:**

   - Analyze where your website and social media traffic is coming from. This helps you identify which platforms and campaigns are driving the most interest and engagement.

4. **Token Holder Growth:**

- Use blockchain explorers and Pump.fun's PumpVision to monitor the growth in the number of token holders. Rapid growth can indicate successful marketing and increased interest in your meme coin.

5. **Liquidity and Trading Volume:**

- Track liquidity levels and trading volumes on both centralized and decentralized exchanges. High liquidity and trading volume suggest a healthy and active market for your meme coin.

Tools for Measuring Impact:

- **PumpVision:** Utilize Pump.fun's PumpVision to access real-time analytics and on-chain data. Track key metrics such as liquidity, trading volumes, and token holder distributions.

- **Google Analytics:** Integrate Google Analytics with your website to monitor traffic sources, user behavior, and conversion rates.

- **Social Media Analytics:** Use built-in analytics tools on platforms like Twitter (X), Discord, Reddit, and Telegram to measure engagement and track the performance of your posts and campaigns.

How to Use the Data:

1. **Identify Successful Strategies:**

- Analyze which promotional strategies are driving the most engagement and conversions. Focus your efforts on these successful tactics to maximize their impact.

2. **Optimize Underperforming Campaigns:**

○ Identify campaigns that are not performing well and make necessary adjustments. This could involve tweaking your messaging, changing your target audience, or experimenting with different content formats.

3. **Make Data-Driven Decisions:**

○ Use the insights gained from analytics to inform your future marketing strategies. For example, if a particular type of content consistently performs well, allocate more resources to creating similar content.

Example Scenario: Suppose you launch a meme contest and track its performance using PumpVision. You notice a significant increase in token holders and trading volume following the contest. Additionally, social media engagement metrics show a spike in likes, shares, and comments. This indicates that the contest was successful in generating genuine interest and driving meaningful engagement. You can then plan to host similar events in the future to continue building hype and community support.

Adhering to Ethical Standards and Regulations

Ensuring Compliance and Building Long-Term Trust

Adhering to ethical standards and regulatory requirements is essential for the long-term success and credibility of your meme coin. By maintaining high ethical standards and ensuring compliance, you build trust with your community and avoid potential legal issues that could jeopardize your project.

Steps to Ensure Compliance:

1. **Understand Regulatory Requirements:**

○ Research the legal requirements for cryptocurrency projects in the jurisdictions where you operate and where your investors are located. This may include anti-money laundering (AML) and know your customer (KYC) regulations.

2. Implement KYC/AML Procedures:

- If necessary, implement KYC/AML procedures to verify the identities of your investors. This helps prevent fraudulent activities and ensures compliance with regulatory standards.

3. Transparent Governance:

- Establish a transparent governance structure for your meme coin. Clearly define decision-making processes, roles, and responsibilities within your team.

4. Regular Audits and Reporting:

- Conduct regular audits of your smart contracts and financial transactions. Publish audit reports and provide regular updates to your community to demonstrate ongoing compliance and commitment to transparency.

5. Ethical Marketing Practices:

- Avoid misleading advertising, exaggerated claims, and manipulative tactics. Focus on honest and transparent communication about your meme coin's features, benefits, and potential risks.

Building Long-Term Trust:

- **Consistency:** Maintain consistent communication and updates with your community. Regularly share progress, milestones, and any changes to the project.

- **Responsiveness:** Be responsive to community feedback and concerns. Address issues promptly and transparently to show that you value your community's input.

- **Integrity:** Uphold high ethical standards in all aspects of your project, from development and marketing to community engagement and financial management.

Benefits of Adhering to Ethical Standards:

- **Enhanced Reputation:** Ethical practices build a positive reputation within the crypto community, attracting more genuine investors and supporters.

- **Legal Protection:** Compliance with regulations helps protect your project from legal issues and potential shutdowns.

- **Sustainable Growth:** Ethical promotion fosters long-term trust and loyalty, ensuring the sustained growth and success of your meme coin.

Pumping your meme coin ethically is about creating genuine excitement and trust without resorting to manipulative or deceptive tactics. By focusing on quality content, transparent communication, ethical influencer partnerships, responsible advertising, and comprehensive risk management, you can build a strong and sustainable meme coin project. Utilizing tools like Pump.fun and PumpVision enhances your ability to promote your project effectively while maintaining transparency and integrity.

For creators, adhering to ethical standards not only protects your project's reputation but also fosters a loyal and supportive community that will drive long-term success. For investors, understanding and recognizing these ethical practices helps you make informed decisions and invest in projects with genuine potential and trustworthy management.

By following the guidelines and strategies outlined in this chapter, you can ensure that your meme coin not only gains visibility and popularity but does so in a way that builds lasting trust and credibility within the cryptocurrency ecosystem. Ethical promotion is the foundation of a successful and respected meme coin, paving the way for sustainable growth and a vibrant, engaged community.

Additional Tips for Ethical Pumping:

- **Educate Your Community:** Provide resources and educational materials to help your community understand the project's value and the broader crypto landscape.

- **Foster Inclusivity:** Encourage diverse participation and ensure that all community members feel welcome and valued.

- **Celebrate Milestones:** Acknowledge and celebrate key milestones with your community, reinforcing the project's progress and achievements.

Resources:

- **Pump.fun:** Explore Pump.fun's features for managing and promoting your meme coin effectively.

- **PumpVision:** Utilize Pump.fun's PumpVision for real-time analytics, liquidity monitoring, and smart contract verification.

- **Blockchain Explorers:** Use Etherscan, BscScan, and other blockchain explorers to verify token authenticity and track transactions.

- **Crypto News Outlets:** Stay updated with the latest trends and developments through reputable sources like CoinDesk, CoinTelegraph, and CryptoSlate.

By integrating these practices and tools into your promotional strategy, you can ethically pump your meme coin, ensuring that your project stands out in a crowded market and attracts a dedicated and trustworthy community.

Chapter 10

Selling and Exiting Your Meme Coin Investments

Investing in meme coins can be highly rewarding, but it also comes with significant risks. As the market for meme coins is notoriously volatile, developing a clear strategy for selling and exiting your investments is crucial to maximizing profits and minimizing losses. This chapter will guide you through the essential steps of creating an exit strategy, monitoring market conditions, executing sell orders, managing taxes, reinvesting profits, securing your earnings, evaluating your investment performance, learning from your experiences, maintaining long-term financial health, and staying engaged with the crypto community post-sale. By leveraging tools like Pump.fun, alongside other essential platforms, you can navigate the complexities of exiting your meme coin investments confidently and ethically.

Developing a Clear Exit Strategy

Setting Profit Targets and Timelines Based on Verifiable Market Conditions

A well-defined exit strategy begins with setting clear profit targets and timelines. This approach helps you make informed decisions and avoid emotional trading, which is often driven by fear or greed.

For Creators and Investors:

1. **Define Profit Targets:**

   ○ **Percentage Gains:** Determine specific percentage gains at which you plan to sell a portion or all of your investment. For example, you might decide to sell 25% of your holdings when the price increases by 50%, another 25% at a 100% gain, and so forth.

   ○ **Dollar Amounts:** Alternatively, set dollar-based targets based on your investment goals. This method is particularly useful if you have a specific financial objective in mind.

2. **Set Timelines:**

   ○ **Short-Term vs. Long-Term:** Decide whether your exit strategy is short-term, targeting quick gains, or long-term, aiming for sustained growth. This depends on your investment horizon and risk tolerance.

   ○ **Market Conditions:** Align your timelines with market cycles. For instance, exiting during a bull market might yield higher returns, while a bear market might require more conservative targets.

3. **Use Verifiable Market Conditions:**

   ○ **Technical Indicators:** Utilize technical indicators such as Moving Averages (MA), Relative Strength Index (RSI), and Bollinger Bands to identify optimal selling points.

   ○ **On-Chain Data:** Leverage tools like Pump.fun's PumpVision to analyze on-chain metrics, including transaction volumes, holder distributions, and liquidity levels, to make data-driven decisions.

Monitoring Market Conditions for Optimal Selling

Using Blockchain Verification and Aggregator Tools to Gauge Liquidity and Sentiment

Staying informed about market conditions is essential for timing your exit effectively. Monitoring liquidity and sentiment helps you understand the broader market dynamics and make strategic decisions.

For Creators and Investors:

1. **Liquidity Analysis:**

   - **Pump.fun's PumpVision:** Use Pump.fun's PumpVision to monitor liquidity pools on various decentralized exchanges (DEXs). High liquidity ensures that large sell orders can be executed without significant price slippage.

   - **Aggregator Tools:** Utilize aggregator platforms like CoinGecko or CoinMarketCap to get a comprehensive view of liquidity across multiple exchanges.

2. **Sentiment Analysis:**

   - **Social Media Monitoring:** Track sentiment on social media platforms using tweet trackers and sentiment analysis tools. Positive sentiment can indicate strong community support, while negative sentiment might signal upcoming declines.

   - **PumpVision's Sentiment Tools:** Leverage Pump.fun's sentiment analysis features to gauge the overall mood of the market regarding your meme coin. This helps in anticipating potential price movements.

3. **Real-Time Data Feeds:**

   - **Blockchain Explorers:** Use blockchain explorers like Etherscan or BscScan to monitor real-time transaction data, large transfers, and wallet activities that could influence price movements.

- **PumpVision's Real-Time Alerts:** Set up real-time alerts on PumpVision for significant changes in liquidity, trading volumes, or large transactions to stay ahead of market trends.

Executing Sell Orders on Exchanges

Step-by-Step Process, Ensuring the Token's Address Matches the Official Contract

Executing sell orders accurately and securely is crucial to protect your investments and ensure that you're trading the legitimate token.

For Creators and Investors:

1. **Choose the Right Exchange:**

   - **Centralized Exchanges (CEXs):** Platforms like Binance, Coinbase, and Kraken offer high liquidity and user-friendly interfaces.

   - **Decentralized Exchanges (DEXs):** Platforms like Uniswap, PancakeSwap, and Solana-based DEXs provide greater control over your transactions and privacy.

2. **Verify the Token's Contract Address:**

   - **Pump.fun's PumpVision:** Use Pump.fun to confirm that the token's contract address matches the official one provided by the project. This prevents trading counterfeit tokens.

   - **Blockchain Explorers:** Cross-check the contract address on blockchain explorers like Etherscan or BscScan to ensure authenticity.

3. **Place the Sell Order:**

   - **Market Order:** Choose a market order if you want to sell immediately at the current market price. This is quick but may result in price slippage.

- **Limit Order:** Opt for a limit order to sell at a specific price or better. This offers price control but may take longer to execute.

- **Using PumpVision:** Utilize Pump.fun's PumpVision to set up and track your sell orders, ensuring they execute as planned.

4. **Confirm the Transaction:**

- **Double-Check Details:** Before finalizing the sale, double-check the order details, including the token amount, price, and contract address.

- **Secure Confirmation:** Ensure the transaction is confirmed on the blockchain. Use PumpVision to verify the transaction status and ensure it has been executed successfully.

Managing Taxes and Financial Reporting

Understanding Tax Implications and Keeping Verifiable Transaction Records

Cryptocurrency transactions, including buying and selling meme coins, have tax implications that vary by jurisdiction. Properly managing taxes and maintaining accurate records is essential to avoid legal issues and ensure financial compliance.

For Creators and Investors:

1. **Understand Tax Obligations:**

- **Capital Gains Tax:** Selling meme coins for a profit may be subject to capital gains tax. The rate depends on your country's tax laws and how long you held the asset.

- **Income Tax:** Airdrops, staking rewards, and other forms of passive income from meme coins may be considered taxable income.

2. **Keep Detailed Records:**

- **Transaction Logs:** Maintain a comprehensive log of all transactions, including dates, amounts, and prices at the time of each trade.

- **Pump.fun's Transaction Tracking:** Use Pump.fun's built-in tracking features to automatically record and categorize your transactions for easy reference.

3. **Use Tax Software:**

- **Crypto Tax Tools:** Utilize specialized tax software like CoinTracker, Koinly, or TurboTax Crypto to calculate your tax obligations accurately.

- **Integration with Pump.fun:** Ensure that Pump.fun integrates with these tax tools to streamline the process of importing transaction data.

4. **Consult a Tax Professional:**

- **Professional Advice:** Seek advice from a tax professional who is knowledgeable about cryptocurrency taxation to ensure compliance and optimize your tax strategy.

Reinvesting Profits Wisely

Diversifying into New Tokens Vetted by Your Established Verification Methods

Reinvesting your profits can help you grow your cryptocurrency portfolio and maximize returns. However, it's important to do so wisely by diversifying into new tokens that have been thoroughly vetted.

For Creators and Investors:

1. **Identify Promising Tokens:**

   ◦ **Research:** Use Pump.fun's PumpVision and other analytical tools to identify new tokens with strong fundamentals, active development, and a growing community.

   ◦ **Verification:** Ensure that new tokens have been verified through on-chain analysis and have undergone security audits.

2. **Diversify Your Portfolio:**

   ◦ **Spread Risk:** Invest in a variety of meme coins and other cryptocurrencies to reduce exposure to any single asset's volatility.

   ◦ **Balance Allocation:** Allocate your investments based on risk tolerance and potential returns. Include a mix of high-risk, high-reward tokens and more stable, established cryptocurrencies.

3. **Leverage Verified Tools:**

   ◦ **Pump.fun's PumpVision:** Utilize PumpVision to analyze new tokens, track their performance, and ensure they meet your investment criteria.

   ◦ **Blockchain Explorers:** Continue to use blockchain explorers to verify the authenticity and security of new tokens.

4. **Stay Informed:**

   ◦ **Market Trends:** Keep up with the latest market trends and developments to identify emerging opportunities for reinvestment.

- **Community Engagement:** Engage with the communities of new tokens to gain insights and assess their potential for long-term success.

Securing Your Profits

Transferring Funds to Secure Wallets or Fiat Accounts

Once you've realized profits from selling meme coins, it's essential to secure these earnings to protect against market downturns and ensure long-term financial stability.

For Creators and Investors:

1. **Transfer to Secure Wallets:**

   - **Hardware Wallets:** Use hardware wallets like Ledger Nano S/X or Trezor Model T to store your cryptocurrencies offline, providing enhanced security against hacking and theft.

   - **Software Wallets:** For more frequent access, use reputable software wallets with strong security features. Ensure you use wallets that support the specific tokens you hold.

2. **Convert to Fiat Currency:**

   - **Exchange Transfers:** Transfer your funds back to a centralized exchange and convert them to fiat currency (e.g., USD, EUR) if you prefer to hold cash.

   - **Bank Transfers:** Withdraw the converted funds to your bank account for added security and accessibility.

3. **Use Pump.fun's Secure Transfer Tools:**

   - **Integration with Wallets:** Utilize Pump.fun's integration with secure wallets to streamline the transfer process, ensuring that all transactions are verifiable and secure.

- ○ **Transaction Verification:** Use PumpVision to confirm that transfers have been executed correctly and that funds are safely stored in your chosen wallet.

Evaluating Your Investment Performance

Analyzing What Worked and What Didn't Through Recorded On-Chain Data

Evaluating your investment performance is crucial for learning from your experiences and improving your future strategies. By analyzing what worked and what didn't, you can refine your approach to investing in meme coins.

For Creators and Investors:

1. **Review Performance Metrics:**

   - ○ **Profit and Loss:** Calculate your overall profit and loss from each investment to understand your financial outcomes.

   - ○ **Return on Investment (ROI):** Measure the ROI for each meme coin to assess their effectiveness in generating returns.

2. **Analyze On-Chain Data:**

   - ○ **Pump.fun's PumpVision:** Use Pump.fun's PumpVision to analyze on-chain data such as transaction volumes, token holder distributions, and liquidity trends.

   - ○ **Blockchain Explorers:** Utilize blockchain explorers to review detailed transaction histories and wallet activities associated with your investments.

3. **Identify Patterns and Trends:**

- **Successful Strategies:** Determine which strategies led to profitable outcomes. This could include specific entry points, timing of sell orders, or engagement with certain communities.

- **Areas for Improvement:** Identify areas where your strategies fell short, such as missing optimal selling points or failing to diversify adequately.

4. **Document Lessons Learned:**

- **Create a Journal:** Maintain a detailed journal of your investment activities, noting what strategies worked well and which ones need adjustment.

- **Share Insights:** If appropriate, share your findings with your community to contribute to collective knowledge and growth.

Learning from Successes and Failures

Refining Strategies, Adopting New Tools and Trackers

Every investment experience, whether successful or not, provides valuable lessons. By learning from your successes and failures, you can continuously improve your investment strategies.

For Creators and Investors:

1. **Refine Your Strategies:**

- **Success Analysis:** Identify the factors that contributed to successful investments and replicate these strategies in future trades.

- **Failure Analysis:** Understand the reasons behind unsuccessful investments and avoid repeating the same mistakes.

2. **Adopt New Tools and Trackers:**

   ○ **Stay Updated:** Continuously explore new tools and technologies that can enhance your investment analysis and decision-making processes.

   ○ **Integrate Advanced Tools:** Incorporate advanced tools like Pump.fun's PumpVision to gain deeper insights and improve your tracking capabilities.

3. **Seek Continuous Education:**

   ○ **Learn from Experts:** Follow industry experts, attend webinars, and participate in crypto communities to stay informed about the latest trends and strategies.

   ○ **Experiment and Adapt:** Be open to experimenting with new investment approaches and adapting based on market changes and new information.

4. **Implement Feedback Loops:**

   ○ **Community Feedback:** Engage with your community to gather feedback on your strategies and learn from their experiences.

   ○ **Personal Reflection:** Regularly reflect on your investment journey to identify personal strengths and areas for growth.

Maintaining Long-Term Financial Health

Sustainable Wealth Management Practices Informed by Historical Blockchain Data

Maintaining long-term financial health requires disciplined wealth management practices and informed decision-making based on historical data and market insights.

For Creators and Investors:

1. Budgeting and Allocation:

- **Allocate Funds Wisely:** Allocate your investment capital across different asset classes, including meme coins, established cryptocurrencies, and other investment vehicles to diversify risk.

- **Emergency Funds:** Set aside a portion of your funds as an emergency reserve to cover unexpected expenses or market downturns.

2. Regular Portfolio Reviews:

- **Assess Performance:** Conduct regular reviews of your investment portfolio to evaluate performance and adjust allocations as needed.

- **Rebalance Holdings:** Periodically rebalance your portfolio to maintain your desired level of diversification and risk exposure.

3. Use Historical Data for Insights:

- **Pump.fun's PumpVision:** Leverage Pump.fun's PumpVision to analyze historical on-chain data, such as past price movements, liquidity trends, and holder distributions, to inform your investment decisions.

- **Trend Analysis:** Identify long-term trends and patterns in the meme coin market to make strategic investment choices.

4. Implement Risk Management:

- **Set Limits:** Define limits on the amount of capital you're willing to risk on individual investments to prevent significant losses.

- **Diversify Investments:** Spread your investments across multiple meme coins and other assets to reduce the impact of any single investment's poor performance.

5. **Plan for Financial Goals:**

  ◦ **Set Long-Term Goals:** Define clear financial goals, such as saving for a major purchase, retirement, or other personal objectives, and align your investment strategies to achieve these goals.

  ◦ **Track Progress:** Use financial tracking tools and Pump.fun's PumpVision to monitor your progress towards your financial goals and make adjustments as needed.

Staying Engaged with the Crypto Community Post-Sale

Continuing to Learn from Alpha Groups and Monitoring Evolving Narratives

Maintaining engagement with the crypto community after exiting your investments is essential for continuous learning and staying updated with the latest developments in the market.

For Creators and Investors:

1. **Join Alpha Groups:**

  ◦ **Exclusive Insights:** Alpha groups provide early access to information, insights, and trading signals that can help you stay ahead in the market.

  ◦ **Networking Opportunities:** Engage with other investors and experts to exchange ideas and strategies.

2. **Monitor Evolving Narratives:**

  ◦ **Stay Informed:** Follow the latest trends, news, and developments in the crypto space to understand how narratives evolve and impact the market.

- **Adapt Strategies:** Use the information gathered from alpha groups and market news to refine your investment strategies and make informed decisions.

3. Participate in Community Discussions:

- **Share Knowledge:** Contribute to community discussions by sharing your experiences and insights. This not only helps others but also reinforces your understanding of the market.

- **Learn from Others:** Gain valuable knowledge from other community members' experiences and strategies.

4. Continuous Learning:

- **Educational Resources:** Utilize educational platforms, webinars, and courses to deepen your understanding of cryptocurrency markets, blockchain technology, and investment strategies.

- **Follow Thought Leaders:** Stay updated by following influential figures in the crypto space who provide valuable insights and analysis.

Selling and exiting your meme coin investments is a critical aspect of cryptocurrency trading that requires careful planning, informed decision-making, and disciplined execution. By developing a clear exit strategy, monitoring market conditions, executing sell orders securely, managing taxes, reinvesting profits wisely, securing your earnings, evaluating your performance, learning from experiences, maintaining long-term financial health, and staying engaged with the crypto community, you can navigate the volatile world of meme coins effectively.

Key Takeaways:

1. **Develop a Clear Exit Strategy:** Define profit targets and timelines based on verifiable market conditions to guide your selling decisions.

2. **Monitor Market Conditions:** Use blockchain verification and aggregator tools like Pump.fun's PumpVision to gauge liquidity and sentiment for optimal selling.

3. **Execute Sell Orders Securely:** Follow a step-by-step process to place market or limit orders, ensuring the token's address matches the official contract to avoid scams.

4. **Manage Taxes and Financial Reporting:** Understand tax implications and keep detailed, verifiable transaction records using tools like Pump.fun.

5. **Reinvest Profits Wisely:** Diversify into new, vetted tokens to spread risk and capitalize on growth opportunities.

6. **Secure Your Profits:** Transfer funds to secure wallets or fiat accounts to protect your earnings from market volatility.

7. **Evaluate Investment Performance:** Analyze what worked and what didn't using recorded on-chain data to refine your strategies.

8. **Learn from Successes and Failures:** Continuously improve by adopting new tools and trackers, and refining your investment approach based on past experiences.

9. **Maintain Long-Term Financial Health:** Implement sustainable wealth management practices informed by historical blockchain data to ensure financial stability.

10. **Stay Engaged with the Crypto Community:** Continue learning from alpha groups and monitoring evolving narratives to stay ahead in the dynamic crypto market.

By following these guidelines and utilizing tools like Pump.fun and PumpVision, both creators and investors can ensure that their meme coin investments are managed ethically, securely, and profitably. The key to success lies in informed decision-making, continuous learning, and maintaining transparency and trust within the community. Whether you're a creator looking to maximize your project's potential or an investor aiming to secure your profits and grow your portfolio, this chapter provides the foundational strategies needed to navigate the complex and exciting world of meme coins effectively.

Additional Resources

- **Pump.fun:** Explore Pump.fun's features for managing and optimizing your meme coin investments.

- **PumpVision:** Utilize Pump.fun's PumpVision for real-time analytics, liquidity monitoring, and smart contract verification.

- **Blockchain Explorers:** Use Etherscan, BscScan, and other blockchain explorers to verify token authenticity and track transactions.

- **Crypto Tax Tools:** Tools like CoinTracker, Koinly, and TurboTax Crypto can help manage tax obligations efficiently.

- **Educational Platforms:** Websites like CoinGecko Academy, Investopedia, and CryptoZombies offer valuable insights into cryptocurrency trading and blockchain technology.

- **Community Forums:** Engage with communities on Reddit, Discord, and Telegram to share experiences and gain knowledge from fellow crypto enthusiasts.

By integrating these resources into your investment strategy, you can enhance your understanding, make informed decisions, and achieve long-term success in the ever-evolving landscape of meme coins.

Appendix

Welcome to the appendices of "From Zero to Meme Coin Hero: A Step-by-Step Playbook for Spotting and Flipping Early-Stage Tokens." This section serves as a comprehensive reference, providing definitions, resources, templates, and best practices to support your journey in the meme coin ecosystem. Whether you're a beginner or looking to refine your strategies, these appendices offer valuable tools and insights to enhance your understanding and effectiveness in the cryptocurrency market.

Glossary of Key Terms

Understanding the terminology is fundamental to navigating the cryptocurrency landscape. This glossary covers essential terms and verification tools you'll encounter.

Airdrop: A distribution method where free tokens are sent to community members' wallets, often used to promote a new cryptocurrency.

Altcoin: Any cryptocurrency other than Bitcoin, including Ethereum, Ripple, and meme coins like Dogecoin.

Blockchain: A decentralized digital ledger that records all transactions across a network of computers. It ensures transparency and security.

BullX: A specialized tool for analyzing and verifying the security and performance of decentralized exchanges (DEXs).

CEX (Centralized Exchange): A cryptocurrency exchange managed by a central authority, such as Binance or Coinbase, where users trade through the platform.

DEX (Decentralized Exchange): An exchange that operates without a central authority, allowing users to trade directly from their wallets. Examples include Uniswap and PancakeSwap.

Liquidity Pool: A collection of funds locked in a smart contract on a DEX, enabling users to trade tokens without needing a traditional order book.

Pump.fun: An integrated platform that offers tools like PumpVision for creating, managing, and analyzing meme coins, focusing on transparency and verification.

PumpVision: A feature within Pump.fun that provides real-time analytics, liquidity monitoring, and smart contract verification for meme coins.

Smart Contract: Self-executing contracts with the terms of the agreement directly written into code. They run on blockchain networks like Ethereum and Solana.

Tokenomics: The economic model and distribution strategy of a cryptocurrency, including total supply, distribution methods, and incentive structures.

Whale: An individual or entity that holds a large amount of a particular cryptocurrency, capable of influencing market prices through significant trades.

Resource List

To succeed in the meme coin market, leveraging the right tools and platforms is essential. Below is a curated list of recommended resources:

Tools:

- **Pump.fun:** Comprehensive platform for creating, managing, and analyzing meme coins. Features PumpVision for real-time analytics and verification.

- **BullX:** Advanced tool for analyzing and securing decentralized exchanges (DEXs). Offers insights into liquidity and smart contract security.

- **BirdEye:** Sentiment analysis tool that monitors social media platforms to gauge community sentiment and detect trends.

- **Cielo:** Blockchain explorer and wallet activity tracker, providing detailed insights into wallet behaviors and transaction histories.

Websites and Platforms:

- **CoinGecko:** Cryptocurrency data aggregator providing real-time prices, market capitalization, and trading volumes.

- **CoinMarketCap:** Another major cryptocurrency data platform offering comprehensive market data and analytics.

- **Etherscan:** Blockchain explorer for the Ethereum network, allowing users to verify token contracts and track transactions.

- **BscScan:** Blockchain explorer for the Binance Smart Chain, similar to Etherscan but focused on BSC tokens.

- **CryptoSlate:** Offers news, data, and analysis on various cryptocurrency projects and market trends.

- **Investopedia:** Educational platform with detailed articles and tutorials on cryptocurrency and blockchain technology.

Sample Checklists

Checklists help ensure you don't miss critical steps in evaluating meme coins, verifying on-chain data, and managing investments.

Checklist for Evaluating Meme Coins:

1. Project Legitimacy:

- Verify the token's contract address on blockchain explorers.

- Check for third-party audit reports.

2. Tokenomics:

- Review the total supply and distribution model.

- Assess the incentive structures (e.g., staking rewards, airdrops).

3. Community Engagement:

- Evaluate the size and activity level of the community on platforms like Discord and Telegram.

- Look for regular updates and transparent communication from the team.

4. Development Activity:

- Check the project's GitHub repository for recent commits and active development.

- Review the roadmap and progress towards milestones.

5. Liquidity:

- Ensure sufficient liquidity on reputable DEXs using tools like PumpVision.

- Analyze trading volumes and liquidity pool stability.

Checklist for Verifying On-Chain Data:

1. Smart Contract Verification:

- Confirm the contract address matches official sources.

- Review audit reports for security vulnerabilities.

2. **Transaction History:**

- Analyze transaction volumes and large transfers using blockchain explorers.

- Monitor wallet activities for suspicious patterns.

3. **Liquidity Pools:**

- Verify liquidity pool sizes and stability on DEXs.

- Check for transparency in liquidity provision and removal.

4. **Holder Distribution:**

- Use tools like PumpVision to assess the distribution of token holdings.

- Identify and monitor large holders (whales) for potential market influence.

5. **Compliance:**

- Ensure the project adheres to regulatory requirements in relevant jurisdictions.

- Verify that the project implements AML/KYC procedures if necessary.

Smart Contract Templates

Creating secure and transparent smart contracts is vital for the success and trustworthiness of your meme coin. Below are basic code snippets for Ethereum and Solana, along with guidance on verifying their authenticity.

Ethereum Smart Contract Template (ERC-20):

solidityCopy code

```
// SPDX-License-Identifier: MIT
pragma solidity ^0.8.0;

import            "@openzeppelin/contracts/to-
ken/ERC20/ERC20.sol";

contract MemeCoin is ERC20 {
        constructor(uint256      initialSupply)
ERC20("MemeCoin", "MEME") {
    _mint(msg.sender,  initialSupply  *  (10  **
uint256(decimals())));
    }
}
```

Guidance on Verification:

1. **Deploying the Contract:**

   ◦ Use a reputable development environment like Remix or Hardhat.

   ◦ Ensure you test the contract thoroughly on a testnet before deploying to the mainnet.

2. **Verification:**

   ◦ Verify the contract on Etherscan by uploading the source code and ensuring it matches the deployed bytecode.

   ◦ Provide the verified contract address to your community for transparency.

3. **Security Audits:**

- Engage a third-party security firm to audit your smart contract.

- Publish the audit report and address any identified vulnerabilities promptly.

Solana Smart Contract Template (SPL Token):

rustCopy code

```
use spl_token::state::Mint;

#[program]pub mod meme_coin {
use super::*;

  pub fn initialize(ctx: Context<Initialize>, ini-
tial_supply: u64) -> ProgramResult {
let mint = &mut ctx.accounts.mint;
  mint.mint_authority = *ctx.accounts.author-
ity.key;
mint.supply = initial_supply;
Ok(())
}
}
```

Guidance on Verification:

1. **Deploying the Contract:**

   - Use the Solana CLI or Anchor framework to deploy your smart contract.

   - Test the contract on a devnet before deploying to the mainnet.

2. **Verification:**

   - Verify the contract using Solana blockchain explorers like Solscan.

○ Ensure the deployed contract matches the source code shared with your community.

3. Security Audits:

○ Conduct thorough security audits with experienced firms specializing in Solana.

○ Share audit results publicly and implement recommended security measures.

Legal and Compliance Resources

Navigating the legal landscape is crucial to ensure your meme coin project adheres to regulations and maintains transparency.

Guides on Understanding and Adhering to Regulations:

1. Anti-Money Laundering (AML) and Know Your Customer (KYC):

○ Implement AML/KYC procedures to verify the identities of your investors and prevent fraudulent activities.

○ Use reputable third-party services like Chainalysis or Jumio for compliance verification.

2. Securities Laws:

○ Determine if your meme coin falls under securities regulations in your jurisdiction.

○ Consult with legal experts to ensure compliance with local and international securities laws.

3. Data Protection:

○ Adhere to data protection regulations like GDPR (General Data Protection Regulation) if operating within the EU.

- Ensure secure handling and storage of personal data collected during KYC processes.

Ensuring Transparent Audits:

1. **Regular Audits:**

   - Schedule regular audits of your smart contracts and financial transactions.

   - Engage reputable auditing firms to perform comprehensive security assessments.

2. **Public Audit Reports:**

   - Publish audit reports on your website and social media channels.

   - Provide summaries of key findings and actions taken to address any vulnerabilities.

3. **Continuous Monitoring:**

   - Use tools like PumpVision to continuously monitor the security and performance of your smart contracts.

   - Implement automated alerts for any suspicious activities or security breaches.

Recommended Legal Resources:

- **Legal Firms Specializing in Crypto:** Engage with law firms that specialize in cryptocurrency regulations, such as **DLx Law** or **Perkins Coie**.

- **Regulatory Bodies:** Stay updated with guidelines from regulatory bodies like the **SEC (Securities and Exchange Commission)** in the U.S., **FCA (Financial Conduct Authority)** in the UK, and similar organizations in other jurisdictions.

- **Online Legal Platforms:** Utilize platforms like **Rocket Lawyer** or **LegalZoom** for initial legal guidance and documentation.

Marketing Plan Templates

Developing a structured marketing plan is essential for promoting your meme coin effectively. Below are frameworks to help you create comprehensive promotional strategies backed by verifiable metrics.

Framework for Developing Promotional Strategies:

1. **Define Your Goals:**

   - **Awareness:** Increase the visibility of your meme coin within the crypto community.

   - **Engagement:** Foster active participation and interaction from your community.

   - **Conversion:** Convert community members into token holders and active traders.

2. **Identify Your Target Audience:**

   - **Demographics:** Age, location, interests, and behavior of your potential investors.

   - **Psychographics:** Motivations, values, and attitudes towards cryptocurrency and meme coins.

3. **Choose Marketing Channels:**

   - **Social Media:** Platforms like Twitter (X), Instagram, TikTok, Discord, and Reddit.

   - **Content Marketing:** Blogs, videos, podcasts, and infographics.

   - **Influencer Partnerships:** Collaborate with reputable influencers and content creators.

4. **Develop Content Strategy:**

   - **Educational Content:** Explain the value proposition, tokenomics, and use cases of your meme coin.

   - **Engaging Content:** Create memes, videos, and interactive posts that resonate with your audience.

   - **Promotional Content:** Announce partnerships, milestones, and special events.

5. **Set Metrics and KPIs:**

   - **Engagement Rates:** Likes, shares, comments, and participation in events.

   - **Conversion Rates:** Number of new token holders, trading volumes, and liquidity additions.

   - **Reach and Impressions:** Total number of people exposed to your marketing messages.

6. **Implement and Monitor:**

   - **Use Tools like Pump.fun:** Leverage Pump.fun's PumpVision to track marketing performance and adjust strategies based on real-time data.

   - **A/B Testing:** Experiment with different content formats and messages to identify what works best.

   - **Regular Reviews:** Conduct monthly reviews of your marketing plan to assess progress and make necessary adjustments.

Sample Marketing Plan Template:

markdownCopy code

Marketing Plan for MemeCoin XYZ

1. Executive Summary: - Brief overview of the project and marketing objectives.

2. Goals and Objectives: - Increase social media following by 50% in 3 months.
  - Achieve $1M in trading volume within 6 months.
- Grow the Discord community to 10,000 active members.

3. Target Audience: - Crypto enthusiasts aged 18-35.
 - Individuals interested in meme culture and digital assets.

4. Marketing Channels: - **Social Media:** Twitter (X), Instagram, TikTok
- **Community Platforms:** Discord, Reddit
  - **Content Marketing:** Blog posts, YouTube videos, TikTok clips

5. Content Strategy: - **Educational:** Weekly blog posts explaining tokenomics and project updates.
 - **Engaging:** Daily memes and interactive polls on Twitter and Instagram.
 - **Promotional:** Monthly giveaways and airdrops to incentivize community participation.

6. Influencer Partnerships: - Partner with 5 crypto influencers with transparent on-chain histories.
 - Execute collaborative campaigns and AMAs with influencers to reach broader audiences.

7. Budget Allocation: - Social Media Advertising: 40%
- Influencer Partnerships: 30%
- Content Creation: 20%
- Community Events and Giveaways: 10%

8. Metrics and KPIs: - Social Media Growth: Track followers, likes, shares, and engagement rates.
 - Trading Volume: Monitor daily and monthly trading volumes.
- Community Growth: Measure active members and participation in Discord and Reddit.
 - ROI: Calculate return on investment for each marketing campaign using PumpVision analytics.

9. Implementation Timeline: - **Month 1-3:** Focus on building social media presence and launching initial marketing campaigns.
- **Month 4-6:** Scale influencer partnerships and increase trading volume through targeted promotions.
- **Month 7-12:** Expand into new marketing channels and optimize strategies based on performance data.

10. Review and Optimization: - Conduct monthly performance reviews using Pump.fun's PumpVision.
- Adjust marketing strategies based on data-driven insights and community feedback.

Community Engagement Strategies

Fostering a strong, engaged community is vital for the success of your meme coin. Here are best practices for building trust, transparency, and activity within your community.

Best Practices for Community Engagement:

1. **Transparent Communication:**

   - Regularly update your community about project developments, milestones, and challenges.

   - Use multiple channels (Discord, Telegram, Reddit) to ensure broad reach and accessibility.

2. **Interactive Content:**

   - Host AMAs, live streams, and Q&A sessions to interact directly with your community.

   - Encourage user-generated content through contests, challenges, and meme creation.

3. **Incentivize Participation:**

   - Offer rewards for active community members, such as exclusive airdrops, staking rewards, or NFTs.

   - Implement referral programs to encourage members to invite new participants.

4. **Build a Supportive Environment:**

  ○ Foster a positive and inclusive atmosphere by moderating discussions and addressing toxic behavior.

  ○ Provide support channels for members to ask questions and seek assistance.

5. **Leverage Alpha Groups:**

  ○ Create exclusive groups for early supporters to access insider information, early token releases, and special events.

  ○ Use these groups to gather feedback and involve them in decision-making processes.

Example Community Engagement Activities:

• **Weekly Challenges:** Host themed challenges that encourage members to create and share content related to your meme coin.

• **Virtual Meetups:** Organize regular virtual events where community members can network, share ideas, and celebrate milestones together.

• **Exclusive Content:** Provide members with exclusive access to behind-the-scenes content, development updates, and early announcements.

Security Best Practices

Protecting your investments and maintaining the integrity of your meme coin requires robust security measures. Here are best practices to safeguard your assets, identify scam patterns, and verify influencer claims.

Best Practices for Protecting Your Investments:

1. **Use Hardware Wallets:**

- Store your meme coins in hardware wallets like Ledger Nano S/X or Trezor Model T to keep them offline and secure from hacking attempts.

- Regularly update your hardware wallet's firmware to ensure it remains secure against new threats.

2. Verify Contract Addresses:

- Always double-check the token's contract address using Pump.fun's PumpVision and blockchain explorers to avoid interacting with counterfeit tokens.

- Share the verified contract address prominently on your website and social media channels.

3. Enable Two-Factor Authentication (2FA):

- Activate 2FA on all your exchange accounts and wallets to add an extra layer of security.

4. Monitor Wallet Activity:

- Use tools like PumpVision to track your wallet's activity and detect any unusual transactions or large transfers that could indicate a security breach.

- Set up alerts for specific activities, such as large outgoing transactions, to respond promptly to potential threats.

Identifying Scam Patterns:

1. Suspicious Transactions:

- Monitor for unusual trading volumes, rapid price movements, or large transactions that could indicate pump-and-dump schemes.

- Use PumpVision's real-time analytics to detect abnormal trading behaviors.

2. **Reused or Fake Social Media Handles:**

   ○ Be cautious of projects with reused or generic social media handles that may impersonate legitimate projects.

   ○ Verify the authenticity of social media accounts through verified badges and cross-referencing with official sources.

3. **Bundling Behavior:**

   ○ Identify multiple related wallets buying tokens in sync, which could suggest coordinated pump activities.

   ○ Use blockchain explorers to analyze wallet behaviors and transactions patterns.

Verifying Influencer Claims:

1. **Check Wallet Holdings:**

   ○ Use PumpVision to verify that influencers hold and have transacted with your meme coin. This demonstrates their genuine support and reduces the risk of paid, non-genuine endorsements.

   ○ Examine influencers' wallet histories to ensure they have a track record of supporting legitimate projects.

2. **Assess Influencer Credibility:**

   ○ Research influencers' past collaborations and their outcomes. Favor those who have consistently supported successful and transparent projects.

   ○ Look for authentic engagement and positive feedback from their followers, indicating genuine influence and trustworthiness.

Case Study Templates

Analyzing real-world examples helps you understand how successful meme coins have navigated the market. Use the following template to analyze case studies, focusing on blockchain verification steps.

Case Study Template:

1. Project Overview:

- **Name:** [MemeCoin Name]

- **Launch Date:** [Date]

- **Blockchain:** [Ethereum/Solana/BSC]

- **Tokenomics:** [Total Supply, Distribution Model, Incentives]

2. Initial Launch:

- **Airdrop Details:** [How tokens were distributed initially]

- **Liquidity Provision:** [Amount and platform used]

- **Initial Marketing Strategies:** [Social media campaigns, influencer partnerships]

3. Growth Strategies:

- **Community Engagement:** [Events, AMAs, contests]

- **Development Milestones:** [Key updates, feature releases]

- **Exchange Listings:** [CEX and DEX listings achieved]

4. Blockchain Verification Steps:

- **Contract Verification:** [Verified on Etherscan/Solana Explorer]

- **Audit Reports:** [Details of security audits conducted]

- **Liquidity Monitoring:** [Tools used like PumpVision for tracking]

5. Marketing and Promotion:

- **Content Strategy:** [Types of content created, engagement metrics]

- **Influencer Collaborations:** [Names, verification methods]

- **Advertising Campaigns:** [Platforms used, ROI metrics]

6. Challenges Faced:

- **Market Volatility:** [How the project handled price fluctuations]

- **Security Issues:** [Any breaches or vulnerabilities addressed]

- **Community Management:** [Handling negative sentiment or disputes]

7. Results and Outcomes:

- **Market Performance:** [Price history, trading volumes]

- **Community Growth:** [Number of active members, engagement rates]

- **Project Milestones Achieved:** [Completed roadmap goals, new partnerships]

8. Lessons Learned:

- **Successful Strategies:** [What worked well and why]

- **Areas for Improvement:** [What could have been done better]

9. Conclusion:

- **Overall Assessment:** [Success factors, sustainability]

- **Future Prospects:** [Next steps, ongoing plans]

Frequently Asked Questions (FAQs)

Addressing common queries helps clarify uncertainties and provides quick answers to pressing questions about verification, scam avoidance, and influencer tracking.

Q1: What is Pump.fun and how can it help me manage my meme coin? A1: Pump.fun is an integrated platform designed to create, manage, and analyze meme coins. It offers tools like PumpVision for real-time analytics, liquidity monitoring, and smart contract verification, ensuring transparency and security for both creators and investors.

Q2: How do I verify the authenticity of a meme coin before investing? A2: Use blockchain explorers like Etherscan or BscScan to verify the token's contract address. Additionally, tools like Pump.fun's PumpVision can provide detailed on-chain data and security audits to ensure the token is legitimate and secure.

Q3: What are the signs of a potential pump-and-dump scheme? A3: Look for sudden spikes in trading volume, large buy orders from multiple related wallets, and aggressive marketing without substantive project updates. Tools like PumpVision can help detect unusual trading patterns and suspicious wallet activities.

Q4: Why is community size important for a meme coin's success? A4: A large and active community drives demand, fosters loyalty, and contributes to the token's visibility and liquidity. Engaged community members are more likely to promote the coin organically and support its growth.

Q5: How can I protect my investments from scams? A5: Use hardware wallets for secure storage, verify contract addresses through blockchain explorers, monitor wallet activities with tools like PumpVision, and stay informed about common scam tactics. Additionally, engage with projects that prioritize transparency and have undergone security audits.

Q6: What should I do if I suspect a meme coin is a scam? A6: Cease all transactions immediately, report the project to relevant platforms and authorities, and alert the community through official channels. Use blockchain explorers to gather evidence of suspicious activities and protect your assets by moving them to secure wallets.

Q7: How do I set up a stop-loss order on an exchange? A7: Navigate to the trading section of your exchange, select the token you wish to sell, choose the stop-loss order option, set the trigger price (the price at which you want to sell), and confirm the order. Tools like PumpVision can help you monitor price levels to set appropriate stop-loss points.

Q8: What are the tax implications of selling meme coins? A8: Selling meme coins may be subject to capital gains tax depending on your jurisdiction. It's essential to keep detailed records of all transactions and consult with a tax professional to understand your obligations and ensure compliance.

Q9: Can influencers affect the price of meme coins ethically? A9: Yes, influencers can positively impact meme coin prices by promoting genuine projects and providing transparent information. Ethical influencer collaborations involve honest endorsements and verifying that influencers hold and support the token through on-chain data.

Q10: How often should I review my investment portfolio? A10: Regularly reviewing your portfolio, such as monthly or quarterly, allows you to assess performance, adjust holdings based on market conditions, and implement risk management strategies to ensure your investments remain aligned with your financial goals.

Navigating the Future of Meme Coins

As we conclude this comprehensive guide, it's essential to recap the key steps and best practices that have been outlined throughout the book. Navigating the world of meme coins requires a blend of strategic planning, continuous learning, and ethical conduct. The future of meme coins and cryptocurrency, in general, is poised for significant advancements, growing regulatory clarity, and a more secure, data-driven trading environment.

Recap of Key Steps and Best Practices

1. **Setting Up on Exchanges:** Create accounts on reputable exchanges, verify token authenticity, and secure your investments.

2. **Developing a Marketing Plan:** Use quality content, leverage social media, engage with communities, and employ ethical promotion strategies.

3. **Identifying Success Indicators:** Assess community size, liquidity, development activity, smart contract security, and tokenomics.

4. **Ethical Pumping:** Promote your meme coin transparently and responsibly, avoiding manipulative schemes.

5. **Selling and Exiting Investments:** Develop clear exit strategies, monitor market conditions, execute sell orders securely, and manage taxes efficiently.

6. **Utilizing Tools:** Leverage platforms like Pump.fun and PumpVision for analytics, verification, and management of your meme coin activities.

7. **Continuous Learning:** Stay engaged with the crypto community, adapt to market changes, and refine your strategies based on data and experiences.

Reinforcing the Importance of Blockchain Verification and Specialized Tools

Blockchain verification is a cornerstone of trust and transparency in the cryptocurrency market. Tools like Pump.fun's PumpVision provide essential insights into token legitimacy, liquidity, and security, enabling both creators and investors to make informed decisions. By integrating blockchain verification into every aspect of your project—from token creation to marketing and investment management—you ensure that your meme coin stands out as a trustworthy and credible asset in a crowded market.

Emphasizing Ethical and Sustainable Growth

Ethical promotion and sustainable growth practices are fundamental to building long-term trust and success in the meme coin space. By prioritizing transparency, fostering genuine community engagement, and adhering to regulatory standards, you create a solid foundation for your project. Ethical practices not only protect your reputation but also attract a loyal and supportive community, essential for the sustained growth and resilience of your meme coin.

Encouraging Continuous Learning and Adaptation

The cryptocurrency landscape is dynamic, with constantly evolving technologies, market trends, and regulatory environments. Continuous learning and adaptation are crucial to staying ahead and maintaining the relevance and competitiveness of your meme coin. Engage with educational resources, participate in alpha groups, and utilize advanced tools to refine your strategies and respond effectively to market changes.

Vision for the Future of Meme Coins and Cryptocurrency

Looking ahead, the future of meme coins and the broader cryptocurrency market is promising, driven by technological advancements, increased regulatory clarity, and a shift towards more secure and data-driven trading practices. Innovations in blockchain technology, such as scalability improvements and enhanced security features, will enable meme coins to offer more robust functionalities and integrate seamlessly into diverse ecosystems.

Growing regulatory clarity will also play a pivotal role in legitimizing meme coins, providing a safer and more predictable environment for investors and creators alike. As regulations become more defined, projects that adhere to compliance standards and prioritize transparency will thrive, attracting institutional investments and fostering greater mainstream acceptance.

Moreover, the integration of advanced analytical tools and blockchain verification methods will empower investors with deeper insights, enabling smarter and more strategic investment decisions. This data-driven approach will mitigate risks, enhance market stability, and promote a more informed and engaged investor community.

In this evolving landscape, meme coins will continue to innovate and capture the imagination of the crypto community, blending humor, creativity, and financial opportunities. By adhering to the principles outlined in this book—ethical promotion, transparency, community engagement, and continuous learning—you position yourself to navigate the future of meme coins successfully and contribute to a vibrant and sustainable cryptocurrency ecosystem.

By utilizing the resources, templates, and best practices outlined in these appendices, you are well-equipped to manage your meme coin investments effectively, promote your projects ethically, and build a secure and thriving presence in the cryptocurrency market. Remember, the key to success lies in informed decision-making, maintaining transparency, and fostering a supportive community that believes in the value and potential of your meme coin.

About Gerry Marrs Publications

Founded in 2013, Gerry Marrs Publications is dedicated to helping readers improve their lives through high-quality, informative books. With a focus on health and fitness, personal finance, income opportunities, and overall life enrichment, Gerry Marrs Publications aims to empower individuals with the knowledge and tools they need to achieve success and well-being. Each title we publish is carefully selected to provide practical guidance, inspire positive change, and support our readers in living healthier, wealthier, and more fulfilling lives.